CHILDREN'S KNOWLEDGE BANK

Volume-I

Acknowledgement

This project of **Children's Knowledge Bank** is not the result of an individual effort but is the product of collective wisdom and experience of specialists in different fields. We have tried to make it as authentic and interesting as possible and for this, help has been taken of well known works of international standards and of national importance. It is not feasible to list all of them but we express our gratitude to the following publications for the help in preparing these volumes.

References

ENGLISH

1. The Giant Book of What Do You Know, The Hamlyn Publishing, London.
2. 365 Things to Know. The Hamlyn Publishing, London.
3. Knowledge, in 10 volumes, G. Britain.
4. The World Atlas of Mysteries, by Francis Hitching Collins, London.
5. Natural Wonders of the World. P.J. Banyard.
6. Collins Children's Encyclopaedia, Nature, by Kenneth Bailey.
7. Junior Science Encyclopaedia, The Hamlyn Publishing, London.
8. A New Answer Book, 2 Volumes, by Marg Elting and Rose Wyler.
9. Questions and Answers, World International Publishing Ltd., Manchester.
10. Tell Me the Answer, by Andrea Bonanni.
11. Charlie Browns Cyclopaedia, 20 volumes, Funk and Wognalls Inc. New York.
12. The Children's Book of Questions and Answers, by Anathony Addison.
13. The Answer Book About You, by Marg Elting and Rose Wyler.
14. The Science Library, 6 volumes, by Robert Scharff.
15. The Illustrated Reference Book of Modern Technology, by James Mitchell.
16. Encyclopaedia Britainnica (Micropaedia), 10 volumes Encyclopaedia Britainnica Inc. London.
17. Encyclopaedia Britainnica (Micropaedia), 20 volumes.
18. The Raintree Illustrated Science Encyclopaedia, 20 volumes.
19. The Marshall Cavendish Illustrated Encyclopaedia of Knowledge, Marshall Cavendish Books, London.
20. Tell Me Why, 6 volumes, by Arkady Leokum, The Hamlyn Publishing, London.
21. How and Why in Science, 5 volumes, by R.G. Lagu, Homi Bhabha Centre, Bombay.
22. Reader's Digest Library of Modern Knowledge, in 3 Volumes.
23. Science Reporter, A CSIR Publication, Rafi Marg, New Delhi.
24. The New Illustrated Encyclopaedia of World History, 2 volumes, William L. Langer.
25. The New Junior World Encyclopaedia, 20 volumes.
26. The University Desk Encyclopaedia, Dutton, Elsevier.
27. The Penguin Encyclopaedia of Places, W.G. Moore.
28. You and Your Health, 3 volumes, Shryock, Swartout.
29. Joy of Knowledge, in 14 volumes, James Mitchell.
30. 'Finding Out' Magazine, Purnell & Sons Ltd., London.
31. Understanding Science Magazine, UK Publication.
32. McGraw Hill Encyclopaedia of Science and Technology, 15 volumes, McGraw-Hill Co., USA.
33. Von Nostrands Scientific Encyclopaedia.
34. The Family Encyclopaedia of Science, Windward.
35. Asimov's Biographical Encyclopaedia of Science and Technology, by Isaac Asimov.
36. Scientific American Magazines.
37. Guinness Book of World Records.
38. Guinness Facts & Feats Series.

हिन्दी

1. भारत के पक्षी : सालिम अली
2. भारतीय पक्षी : कुवंर सुरेश सिंह
3. भारत का वन्य जीव : ई.पी.जी., अनु. विराज. एम. ए.

Apart from the above reference books, help has been taken from many English and Hindi Books, Dictionaries and Government approved technical glossaries.

CHILDREN'S
KNOWLEDGE BANK (Volume I)

BY

Dr. Sunita Gupta Ph.D. (Phy. Chemistry)
Dr. Neena Agrawal M.B.B.S.

Advisory Board

Dr. C.L. Garg M.Sc., Ph.D.
Scientist, Defence Science Centre,
Ministry of Defence, Government of India
(Chief Advisor)

Dr. Padam Gupta M.B.B.S.
R.K. Gupta M.Sc. (Mathematics)

Pustak Mahal®
DELHI • MUMBAI • BANGALORE • PATNA • HYDERABAD

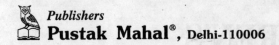

Publishers
Pustak Mahal®, Delhi-110006

Sales Centres
- 6686, Khari Baoli, Delhi-110006, *Ph:* 23944314, 23911979
- 10-B, Netaji Subhash Marg, Daryaganj, New Delhi-110002
  Ph: 23268292, 23268293, 23279900 • *Fax:* 011-23280567
  E-mail: rapidexdelhi@indiatimes.com

Administrative Office
J-3/16 (Opp. Happy School), Daryaganj, New Delhi-110002
Ph: 23276539, 23272783, 23272784 • *Fax:* 011-23260518
E-mail: info@pustakmahal.com • *Website:* www.pustakmahal.com

Branch Offices

BANGALORE : 22/2, Mission Road (Shama Rao's Compound),
Bangalore-560027, *Ph:* 22234025 • *Fax:* 080-22240209
E-mail: pmblr@sancharnet.in • pustak@sancharnet.in

MUMBAI : 23-25, Zaoba Wadi (Opp. VIP Showroom), Thakurdwar,
Mumbai-400002, *Ph:* 22010941 • *Fax:* 022-22053387
E-mail: rapidex@bom5.vsnl.net.in

PATNA : Khemka House, 1st Floor (Opp. Women's Hospital), Ashok Rajpath,
Patna-800004, *Ph:* 3094193 • *Telefax:* 0612-2302719
E-mail: rapidexptn@rediffmail.com

HYDERABAD : 5-1-707/1, Brij Bhawan, Bank Street, Koti,
Hyderabad-500095, *Ph:* 24737530 • *Fax:* 040-24737290
E-mail: pustakmahalhyd@yahoo.co.in

I.S.B.N. 81-223-0289-0

15th Edition : October 2004

Printed at : Param Offsetters, Okhla, New Delhi-110020

Publishers' Note

We are pleased to present this totally new and revised edition of **Children's Knowledge Bank**. The overwhelming response to our earlier edition is what set us about the task of improving and updating the volume in your hand. The edition is a little behind schedule but it is essentially owing to our constant endeavour to bring the reader absolutely the latest and authentic information. In over-all presentation too the edition has undergone major changes. It has also been made more exhaustive and contains seven sections viz., *General Knowledge, Science & Technology, Plants & Animals, Human Body, Earth Science, The Universe* and *Scientists & Inventions.*

In fact the present project had been conceived and created with the specific purpose of satisfying the inherent curiosity of a child to provide answers to his basic queries – the **'hows'**, **'whys'** and **'whats'** that rise in his mind from time to time. For this purpose the language has been especially kept simple and lucid, and the contents are backed by lively illustrations. All this, of course, could not have been possible but for the painstaking and sincere efforts of our editorial and art department for which we are thankful to them.

Initially the work was conceived as an encyclopedic series with four volumes. But as we embarked upon the project we found it difficult to limit its scope. Because after all, is there any end to a child's queries? And if we wished to make it truly a treasure house for the children we had to include more and more. As a result the series got expanded to six volumes. Our basic objective, however is not to just supply information, but to kindle the curiosity, to provide the spark to illuminate a child's mind.

We sincerely hope that the revised edition would prove even more useful and satisfactory to the reader, because our greatest reward lies only in your satisfaction.

— *Publishers*

Contents _____

A Glimpse of Questions Answered in
CHILDREN'S KNOWLEDGE BANK Vol. II
Divided into six sections it deals with 157 questions

Section I — General Knowledge
- What is Multimedia?
- What is FM transmission?
- What is Darwin's theory of evolution?
- Who was Socrates?
- Who is called 'The Lady with the Lamp'?
- How are valleys formed?'
- What is a Hydrogen Bomb?
- When did people first use money?
- What is a Dragon?
- What is Internet?
- Why can't we fly like birds?
- How are submarines detected under the sea?
- Do some plants eat insects?
- Who created the Frankenstein's monster?
- What is Electronic Mail?
- What is Paging Service?
- How can we test the purity of milk?
- How is the distance of stars from the earth measured?
- Which animals resemble man?
- What is a space suit?
- What is a Silicon Chip?
- How fast can marine animals swim?
- What is a flying fish?
- Why do giraffes have a long neck?
- What are pain relievers?
- How does a currency counting machine work?
- Which planets have satellites?
- Why do objects appear coloured?
- Does a black cat bring bad luck?
- How is soil formed?
- How can we reach the bottom of the sea?
- Does any metal exist in a liquid state?
- How is aluminium obtained from the earth?
- What is diamond?
- How is iron obtained from the earth?
- Why does the leaning Tower of Pisa not fall?
- What is a mirage?
- What causes ocean currents?
- When was the construction of bridges started?
- What causes tides in the sea?
- Why does bread have pores?
- How does snowfall occur?
- How is the depth of the sea measured?
- What is fire?
- Who was Alexander the Great?
- What is smoke?
- How are icebergs formed?
- Why does the size of the moon appear to change?
- Why does wind blow?
- Why do we perspire?
- Why do we resemble our parents?
- Why do women have a sweet voice?

Section II — Science & Technology
- How does a microwave oven work?
- Why do stars twinkle?
- What are radio waves?
- How does a pressure cooker work?
- Which material does not burn in fire easily?
- How are millions of substances made from only a few elements?
- What are infra-red radiations?
- What is pasteurization?
- How is weather forecast made?
- How does sound travel?
- Why are all the heavenly bodies round?
- What are the different states of matter?
- How does a thermos flask work?
- What are asteroids?
- What are the wonders of X-Rays?
- Can matter be converted into energy?
- What is the structure of an atom?
- Why can't we see stars during the day?
- Why does thunder follow lightning?
- Why does iron get rusty?
- How does a microscope work?
- What is a nuclear reactor?
- What are nebulae?
- What is electromagnetism?
- Why does the sky appear blue?
- How do we find direction in the sea?
- How is light produced by an electric bulb?
- What are the different forms of energy?
- How is glass made?
- What are constellations?

Section III — Plants & Animals
- How did life begin on earth?
- What is the difference between fruits and vegetables?
- How does a chameleon change its colour?
- Which medicines are obtained from animals?
- How fast can animals run?
- How do bees make honey?
- Why do elephants have trunks?
- Why are some fruits sweet while others are sour?
- How do we estimate the age of a tree?
- Why do flowers have fragrance?
- Why do camels have humps?
- Why do trees shed their leaves?
- Why don't spiders get caught in their own webs?
- What are mammals?
- Why insect bites are dangerous?
- Why is the colour of leaves green?
- How do fish breathe inside water?
- How are bats different from birds?
- How does a wall lizard get rid of its tail?
- How does a firefly glow at night?
- Which are the warm and cold-blooded creatures?
- Can animals identify different colours?
- Why is lion called the king of the beasts?

Section IV — Human Body
- What determines the sex of a child?
- Why do we feel hungry?
- Why do we hiccup?
- Why do we get tired?
- How are we able to speak?
- How do the ears detect sound?
- How do female mammals produce milk?
- Why is the blood red?
- Why do tears come out while weeping?
- How is our body temperature maintained?
- What makes people sneeze?
- How is urine formed in our body?
- Why do some people snore during sleep?
- How do we breathe?
- Why does the human skin have different colours?
- What is roundworm infestation?
- Why does the blood group vary from person to person?
- Why is one of our feet bigger than the other?
- Why do some people become deaf?
- Why do we feel thirsty?
- How do intoxicants affect our body?
- What is pulmonary tuberculosis?
- How are twins born?
- How do we digest food?
- Why are some people left-handed?
- What causes pneumonia?
- Why does our body stop growing after a certain age?
- How does the nose detect smell?
- Why is cutting of nails and hairs painless?
- What causes headaches?
- What are the common eye disorders?
- How does the intake of salt help our body?
- How do muscles work?

Section V — Scientists & Inventions
- Why is Newton called the Father of Physics?
- How did Archimedes detect impurity in the golden crown?
- How was wheel invented?
- What was discovered by Enrico Fermi?
- Who discovered radium?
- Why is Einstein called the greatest scientist of the 20th century?
- Why is Galileo called a great scientist?
- Why is Edison called the Inventor of Inventors?

Section VI — Sports & Entertainment
- What is Sumo wrestling?
- Who is called the Black Pearl ?
- What is Figure Skating?
- When did people start playing cards?
- Where did the game of chess originate?
- Why was Dhyan Chand called the Hockey Wizard?
- What is Kabuki?
- Why is Dada Saheb Phalke award given?
- Who created Mickey Mouse?
- Who was Mozart?
- How do parrot and myna speak like us?

Big size 176 Pages   Fully Illustrated

A Glimpse of Questions Answered in
CHILDREN'S KNOWLEDGE BANK Vol. III
Divided into six sections it deals with 153 questions

Section I—General Knowledge
- Is there any hill that changes its colour ?
- Which are the great mountain ranges of the world?
- Where is Angkor Wat — the largest temple?
- How would you put out a fire ?
- Why shouldn't we watch television in a darkened room ?
- Who was Picasso ?
- How is the rainfall measured ?
- Where did Gypsies come from ?
- Where does wax go from a burning candle?
- What are Calories ?
- How was coal formed?
- How is milk turned into curds ?
- Why was the Eiffel Tower built ?
- What is China clay ?
- Why is Bermuda Triangle so mysterious ?
- Why is Netherlands called the Land of Windmills ?
- What are fossils ?
- What is acupuncture ?
- Why is the Ganges considered sacred ?
- What are the lightest and the heaviest metals ?
- Why do we cup our hands around ourmouth when we call someone ?
- Why doesn't frozen food get spoiled ?
- Why does the flame always rise upwards ?
- What is friction ?
- Where is the International Court of Justice ?
- What are the main classical dances of India ?
- What are the latitudes and longitudes?
- Why don't oil and water mix ?
- Why is electric shock dangerous ?
- Which language has the greatest number of words ?
- How is sulphur obtained ?
- Where is the Death Valley ?
- How is pollution harmful to us ?
- Why does a dead body float on water ?
- Where is World Bank ?
- Do hair really grow even after a person is dead?
- Why do we dream ?
- Does everyone have unique fingerprints ?
- Why don't all nations have one currency ?
- Why do we use fertilizers ?
- Why do we call 1st April a Fools' day ?
- Why was the Taj Mahal built ?
- What is a Light Year?
- How did the continents originate ?
- How is atmospheric pressure measured ?
- Why don't all planets have an atmosphere ?
- What is Disneyland ?
- What are the polar regions ?
- What are the different kinds of fuels ?
- What is inflation ?
- Why do we pay taxes ?

Section II—Plants & Animals
- How did animals get their names ?
- Why do some animals chew their cud ?
- Is there life on other planets ?
- Why do snakes shed their skins ?
- Do plants also breathe ?
- What is a flying fox ?
- What are the magical qualities of garlic ?
- Can a squirrel really fly ?
- Is there any animal which commits suicide ?
- Does the vampire bat feed on blood ?
- Why is a dog's sense of smell better than that of ours ?
- Why do rabbits have large ears ?
- What is a coral ?
- Which animal never drinks water in its entire life?
- How does an insect breathe ?
- When did plants appear on the earth ?
- How useful is the banana ?
- What is a sea-horse ?
- What were the dinosaurs?
- Can a snake swallow an animal whole?

Section III—Inventions & Discoveries
- Who invented the shoes?
- Who discovered Australia ?
- How did the circus begin ?
- When was the stethoscope invented ?
- Who developed the shorthand ?
- How was geometry invented ?
- How did weapons come into use ?
- When was the first light house built ?
- How were the explosives developed ?
- How did the English language originate?
- Where did democracy originate ?
- Who started the kindergarten ?
- When were the museums started ?

Section IV—Modern Science
- How are perfumes made ?
- How does a tape recorder work ?
- What are sulfa drugs ?
- What are alloys ?
- What are isotopes ?
- How does a transformer work ?
- How can we test the purity of pure ghee ?
- Who was the first man to land on the Moon ?
- How is cement made ?
- What are communications satellites ?
- What are cosmic rays ?
- What is a planetarium ?
- How is paper made ?
- How does a fluorescent light work ?
- What are holograms ?
- What is a lie detector ?
- What are laser beams ?
- Can air be converted into a liquid ?
- What is a test-tube baby ?
- How does a soap clean things ?
- How does an electron microscope work ?
- How does a photostat machine work ?

- What is solar energy ?
- How do we take a photograph with a camera ?
- What is a dry cell ?
- How does an airconditioner work ?
- How does a refrigerator work ?
- How does a vacuum cleaner work ?
- Can one element be changed into another ?
- What are video games ?

Section V—Human Body
- What is our body made of ?
- What causes a heart attack ?
- How do we get pimples ?
- How do we see different colours ?
- What causes common cold ?
- What makes the blood clot ?
- What is the function of tonsils ?
- What is saliva ?
- What are hormones ?
- Why does our hair turn grey ?
- Why does our skin wrinkle ?
- How do the blind read and write ?
- What are our teeth ?
- Why is skeleton necessary for us ?
- What elements constitute the human body ?
- Why are vaccinations necessary?
- What is a phobia ?
- Which language is used by deaf-mutes ?
- What is cancer ?
- How does our brain work ?
- Why do our eyes blink ?
- What is the function of the kidneys ?
- What is epilepsy ?
- What causes a peptic ulcer ?
- How is pus formed ?
- Why do we feel sleepy after a heavy meal ?
- What is food poisoning ?
- What is a pacemaker?
- What is Positron Emission Technology ?

Section VI—Sports & Entertainment
- Which is the oldest game in the world ?
- Where did the game of basketball originate ?
- What is marathon ?
- When did rowing begin ?
- Who have been some of India's great sportspersons ?
- What are the popular games of India ?
- When was swimming included as a sport ?
- When did mountaineering become a sport ?
- What is Ballet ?
- What is Jazz ?
- Did Sherlock Holmes really exist?
- What is show-jumping ?
- How did cinema commence ?

Big size 176 Pages   Fully Illustrated

A Glimpse of Questions Answered in
CHILDREN'S KNOWLEDGE BANK Vol. IV
Divided into six sections it deals with 150 questions

Section I—General Knowledge

- When did the first alphabets appear?
- How do astronauts walk in space?
- What is Nitrogen Cycle?
- When did the first Indian Empire arise?
- When was the first artificial satellite launched?
- What are blackholes?
- When was the Sahara desert covered by Ice?
- How many stars can we count at night?
- How do deep-sea divers operate?
- Who was Plato?
- What was the Ice Age?
- What is weightlessness?
- Why is it harder to walk uphill than downhill?
- Why does the Mediterranean Sea appear blue and the Atlantic ocean green?
- What is the United Nations?
- Did ancient people sail across the oceans?
- What is the mystery of sphinx?
- Why do woollen cloths kept in boxes get holes?
- Why are Ajanta and Ellora caves famous?
- Who was Napoleon?
- How far can we see on the surface of the earth?
- What are Auroras?
- What are ultraviolet rays?
- Why is ship's speed measured in knots?
- When was petrol first produced?
- Who was Confucius?
- When were the first towns built?
- What is a litmus paper?
- What is a kaleidoscope?
- What is magnetism?
- Who was Kalidasa?
- Which cities are built on canals?
- Who was the founder of Din-i-Ilahi?
- What are proteins?
- Why is Khajuraho famous?
- What are the two houses of parliament?
- What is Ionosphere?
- Which is the land of midnight sun?
- What is a sextant?
- Why do soldiers salute?
- When were the stupas of Sanchi built?
- How is the altitude of flying aeroplanes determined?
- What are the underground rivers?
- How did different countries get their names?
- What is a Catalyst?
- How did the Egyptians preserve mummies?
- What are the artificial sweetening agents?
- Why is Panama Canal famous?
- What do AM and PM mean?
- How did different superstitions begin?
- How does water become cool in an earthen pitcher?
- What is an Electric fuse?
- When did the industrial revolution begin?

Section II — Science and Technology

- What is a Robot?
- What are Quarks?
- How does a film projector work?
- What is an atomic clock?
- What is heavy water?
- What is stereophonic sound?
- Can light travel through wires?
- How does a polaroid camera take instant photographs?
- What are quasars?
- What is a mass spectrograph?
- What are guided missiles?
- How does a microphone work?
- What is dry cleaning?
- How are different dyes made?
- Why do some acids cause burn?
- What are the different types of thermometers?
- How can the temperatures of stars be measured?
- How are matches made?
- How does a video taperecorder work?
- How are hard drinks made?
- What is a periscope?
- What is quartz?
- How does a automobile engine work?
- How is talcum powder made?
- How is electricity conducted through wires?
- How is an automobile's speed measured?
- How does a crane work?
- How is Nylon made?
- What is the Theory of Relativity?
- How can we extinguish fires?
- How do we see distant objects with binoculars?

Section III — Plant & Animals

- Does any animal wash its food?
- Which sea animals emit light?
- How do birds hear?
- How do aquatic animals survive in frozen lakes and ponds?
- Do insects have blood?
- Which plants feed on other plants?
- Which are the roots we eat?
- Why do insects get attracted towards light?
- Why does peacock display its feathers?
- Which insects have the longest lifespan?
- Which are the different oils extracted from sea?
- Why don't leaves get heated in sunlight?
- How do insects reproduce and develop?
- What are the different types of rhinoceros?
- Which is the most dangerous bird in the world?
- Why do woodpeckers peck the trees?
- Which is the world's deadliest animal?
- Why do flies rub their legs together?
- Which are the large-sized flying birds?
- How can dogs be dangerous to us?

Section IV — Human Body

- What happens in our brain?
- Why do some people stammer?
- What are enzymes?
- Why do doctors examine the pulse?
- Why do babies cry so much?
- What is Typhoid?
- What are the different joints in our body?
- Why are head injuries dangerous?
- What is blood pressure?
- Why do some people have a squint?
- When were the anaesthetics first used for operation?
- What is immunity?
- What causes asthma?
- What is the iron-lung machine?
- What is physiotherapy?
- Why are infants kept on milk?
- What are the functions of arteries and veins in our body?
- What is Chicken pox?
- What is electrocardiography?
- Why people don't have identical voices?
- What causes leprosy?
- What is the function of liver in our body?
- What do we mean by right-eyed or left-eyed people?
- What is allergy?
- What is blood cancer or leukemia?

Section V — Scientists and Inventions

- Who invented zero?
- When were the early hospitals established?
- When was the elevator invented?
- Why was C.V. Raman awarded the Nobel prize?
- Who is known as the Father of Medicine?
- Which discovery made Hargovind Khurana famous?
- Who made the first milking machine?
- Who made the first artificial limbs?

Section VI — Sports & Entertainment

- What are Olympic Games?
- Where did the game of badminton originate?
- What is surfing?
- How old is the game of billiards?
- What is Pentathlon?
- What is Pelota game?
- What are walking races?
- Why is Hollywood famous?
- What are Oscar Awards?

Big size 176 Pages   Fully Illustrated

A Glimpse of Questions Answered in
CHILDREN'S KNOWLEDGE BANK Vol. V
Divided into six sections it deals with 152 questions

Section I—General Knowledge
- What is a Computer Virus?
- What is Carbon Dating?
- How does a hovercraft work?
- How does an airplane stay up in the air?
- Can we measure intelligence?
- Who was Aristotle?
- Where do people live on boats?
- How do traffic lights work?
- What are the different types of calculators?
- What is Bonsai?
- What is Guerrilla Warfare?
- Where is the Big Ben?
- What is a Cosmic Year?
- What is the legend behind the Trojan Horse?
- When was the United Kingdom formed?
- What is a boomerang?
- What is the Food Chain?
- What is the International Date Line?
- How was the Grand Canyon formed?
- Who were the Incas?
- How does a steering wheel make a car turn?
- How can we locate the North Star?
- When did the scout movement begin?
- Who was Columbus?
- What are whispering galleries?
- What was the Stone Age?
- What are pesticides?
- Where is the highest railway line in the world ?
- Where is the Alhambra?
- How did the use of Christmas trees begin?
- What is a semaphore?
- Why is Egypt called the Gift of the Nile?
- Who was Gautama Buddha?
- What is a rain forest?
- What is ozone gas?
- Why do forward moving wheels sometimes appear turning backwards?
- How is cheese made?
- What are the methods of sewage disposal?
- What is a poison?
- What is an avalanche?
- Where did ice-cream originate from?
- What was the French Revolution?
- What is Fool's Gold?
- What is a Theodolite?
- Which is the oldest city in the world?
- What is the black magic of witch doctors?
- Which is the largest river in the world?
- What is Palmistry?
- What is Opera?
- Why is Shakespeare regarded as the world's greatest poet and playwright?
- What are the different types of mirrors?
- What are solar flares?
- Which British Sovereign had the longest reign?
- What is the weight of our atmosphere?
- Where does all the garbage go?
- What is a Chemical Warfare?

Section II—Science & Technology
- What are Novae and Supernovae?
- How does a jet engine work?
- Why does a ship float on water?
- What is Doppler Effect?
- How do detergents perform the cleaning action?
- What is an ammeter?
- What is the science of ballistics?
- What is a welding torch?
- How do we measure the hardness of materials?
- What are the different abrasives?
- What is a clinometer?
- What is electroplating?
- How do satellites stay up in space?
- How is sulphuric acid manufactured?
- What is light?
- How does a siren produce sound?
- How are metals anodized?
- How does a turbine work?
- How does a battery torch work?
- How does a screw jack work?
- Why is 'pi' (π) such a unique number?
- What are the contact lenses?
- How are different paints made?
- What is a shadow?
- What is a Range Finder?
- How does a siphon work?
- How fast do the objects fall?
- What is the refraction of light?
- How does a parachute work?
- What is a prime number?
- What is Electricity?
- What is a pyrometer?
- What is solar wind?

Section III—Plants and Animals
- Do some plants also move?
- Can one tree produce the fruit of a different tree?
- Why do plants and animals become extinct?
- How do we study the internal structure of plants?
- How do some animals recognise their offspring?
- Why do cats purr?
- Which insects swim upside-down?
- Can the fishes hear?
- Which birds cannot fly?
- Why do birds sing?
- Does any bear wear 'glasses'?
- Which lizard squirts blood from its eyes?
- Can a scorpion kill a man?
- Which fish keeps its eggs in its mouth?
- Why are stripes a boon to the zebras?
- How did the first bird evolve?
- How do the plant seeds get dispersed?
- How do the fishes smell things?
- Which are the birds of prey?
- Who is called the king of fishes?
- How did different plants get their names?
- Which animal spends its life upside down?
- Which animals are extinct now?
- How do plants and animals defend themselves?
- How is Nightingale distinct from other birds?
- Why are crocodiles so dangerous?

Section IV—Human Body
- What is Extrasensory Perception?
- What is LSD?
- Why is it said: An apple a day keeps the doctor away?
- What are tranquillizers?
- What causes a reflex action?
- What are emotions?
- What is Electroencephalography (EEG)?
- Why do we shiver on a cold day?
- What are the different methods of birth control?
- Why do we get 'Pins and Needles'?
- What are the different mental illnesses?
- Why do we have a belly button?
- What is anaemia?
- How does our nervous system function?
- What is cirrhosis of the liver?
- What is the Rh factor?
- What is electroshock therapy?
- What is jaundice?
- How is sunlight beneficial for us?
- When did the first human heart transplant take place?
- How does a human baby grow inside its mother's womb?
- What are goose pimples?

Section V—Scientists and Inventions
- Who is called the Father of Modern Chemistry?
- When was Morse code first used?
- How is S.N. Bose associated with Einstein?
- What is gyroscope and who invented it?
- Who is called the Father of Indian Nuclear Science?
- Who is known as the Father of Indian Space Research ?
- What is Shanti Swarup Bhatnagar Award?
- What were Sir J. C. Bose's contributions to science?
- How was the ballpoint pen invented?

Section VI—Sports & Entertainment
- What is the sport of Fencing ?
- How is the game of Table Tennis played?
- What is Hang Gliding?
- When did the sport of Weightlifting begin?
- Who was Marlyn Monroe?
- Who were the Beatles?

Big size   176 Pages   Fully Illustrated

A Glimpse of Questions Answered in
CHILDREN'S KNOWLEDGE BANK Vol. VI
Divided into six sections it deals with 156 questions

Section I—General Knowledge
- What is Artificial Intelligence?
- Why was the Statue of Liberty built?
- Why does Mars appear red?
- Who was the founder of the United States of America?
- What is PIN Code System?
- Where is the world's oldest underground railway?
- Who's brighter: Girls or Boys?
- Can fresh water be obtained from the sea?
- Why were the pyramids of Egypt built?
- What is the Mafia?
- Why does the rising or setting sun appear bigger?
- What are different National Awards?
- Why is the cotton plant called Daughter of the Sun?
- Why are there only ten numbers with single figures?
- How was Suez Canal built?
- Why do we need a passport for going abroad?
- What are political parties and pressure groups?
- What are our National Emblem and National Flag?
- Why are some deserts getting bigger?
- How is flood caused?
- What is First Aid?
- Why does milk spill out when boiled?
- Why is it difficult to see things immediately when we enter a dark room?
- How does wool keep us warm?
- Why do people get married?
- What are Five Year Plans?
- How do we get common salt?
- How was the Giant's Causeway formed?
- What is Ikebana?
- Why was the First World War fought?
- Why are some people tattooed?
- What are the Stone Towers of Arizona?
- Who built the giant statues of Easter Island?
- How can you find out date with the help of stars?
- What are the seas of the moon?
- How do ice columns grow inside caves?
- What is the absolute zero?
- Why does sound change continuously when a vessel is filled up with tap water?
- What is Ceramics?
- How can we use the internal heat of Earth?
- What is a Black Box?
- What is Carbon Cycle?
- How heavy loads are lifted by pulleys?
- What are fuel gases?
- Why are there three pins in a plug?
- What is a CAT scanner?
- What are Antifreeze Compounds?
- What are Mercenaries?
- How did the practice of shaking hands begin?
- What were the main causes of the Second World War?
- What is the Metric System ?
- What are our Fundamental Rights?
- What is UNESCO?

- What are precious stones ?
- What are the functions of the Supreme Court of India ?
- What are luminescent materials ?
- How is vinegar made ?
- How is the President of India elected ?
- What are Kepler's laws of planetary motion ?

Section II—Science & Technology
- What is Greenhouse Effect?
- How does a hair drier work?
- How does a video telephone work?
- How does a motorcycle engine work?
- What is a Bolometer?
- What is a space shuttle?
- Why does camphor change into gas without turning into a liquid first?
- How is sugar made?
- How does an escalator work?
- How does a wet battery work?
- What is interference of light?
- How is electricity transmitted over long distances?
- What is a lathe machine?
- How does a water pump function?
- What is Bernoulli's Effect?
- What is Quantum Theory?
- What are cathode rays?
- How are acoustically sound buildings designed?
- How does a colour television function?
- How does a sodium lamp work?
- What is a Hydrofoil?
- How does a camera's flashlight work?
- What is Liquid Crystal Display?
- What is an embossing machine?
- How do you distinguish between force, work, energy and power?
- What is ammonia gas?
- How do a mixer and grinder work?
- How is wax made?
- How does an electric fan function?
- How do electrically heated appliances work?
- Where would a ball fall when thrown inside a running train?
- What is Osmosis?
- How do trawlers fish?
- How does an Electric Bell function?

Section III—Plants and Animals
- Why do animals have a tail?
- Why do trees change colour in autumn?
- Do snakes love music?
- Which is the most beautiful reptile?
- Which are the largest and smallest flowers?
- Where is cocoa grown?
- Does any animal have three eyes?
- Why do flowers of Raat Ki Rani bloom only at night?
- Why do dogs pant in summer?
- Where do crabs climb trees?
- Which is the largest seabird?
- Which animal can see with its eyes closed?
- How do living beings adapt to their environment?

- How do animals release their tension?
- How do different animals move?
- How do plants protect themselves from frost?
- Which fish spits at insects?

Section IV—Human Body
- What is cholesterol?
- What is consciousness?
- Which substances work as fuel in our body?
- What is electroretinogram?
- Why do we see stars when hit on the head or eyes?
- Why do we belch?
- What is arthritis?
- Does our body have a built-in-clock?
- How are cells, tissues, organs and systems formed in the body?
- Why do we feel pain?
- What causes an itch?
- Does everybody have a different smell?
- What is appendicitis?
- Does our body generate electricity?
- What are the functions of the pancreas?
- What is Electromyogram?
- How is artificial insemination done?
- What causes ringworm?
- How is fluoride useful to our teeth?
- What are hereditary diseases?
- Why do our hands and lips get chapped in cold days?
- How is vision tested?
- What causes influenza?
- What is genetics?
- Who discovered vitamins?
- What is ecology?

Section V—Scientists and Inventions
- When were the guns first made?
- Who was Aryabhatta?
- What were Marconi's contributions to science ?
- Who discovered neutrons?
- Who invented Seismograph?
- Who was Pythagorus?
- What were Ramanujan's contributions to mathematics?
- What are Dr. S. Chandrasekhar's contributions to astrophysics?
- When was the first balloon flight made?

Section VI—Sports & Entertainment
- What is Decathlon?
- What is the game of Golf?
- Who was Charlie Chaplin?
- What are Asian Games?
- What is the sport of karate?
- How is kho-kho played?
- Who were Laurel and Hardy?
- What are the seven notes of music?
- Why is Satyajit Ray called a legend in Indian Cinema?
- Who founded the city of Rome?
- Who was Beethoven?

Big size 176 Pages   Fully Illustrated

1
General Knowledge

• Why does ice float on water ? • How is dust useful to us ? • What is hypnotism ? • How is the rainbow formed ? • Why is gold so costly ? • Are the molecules of all substances in motion ? • Why do watches have jewels ? • How did America get its name ? • What is Red Cross and how was it born ? • Why was the Great Wall of China built? • What is Nobel Prize ? • How is dew formed ? • Why do hot things burn us ? • How is silicon useful to us ? • How is liquid converted into vapour ? • How is oxygen useful to us ? • Why is the census taken ? • What is helium ? • How is copper useful to us ? • How do we get wool from sheep ? • How are the pearls formed ? • When did the postal system start? • Why does the rising and setting Sun appear red ? • What is rubber ? • How was the calendar started ? • How did arithmetic originate ? • Where have the Seven Wonders of the World gone ? • What is echo ? • How did the various religions originate ? • Why and when was the police system started ? • How were the weekdays named ? • Which is the smallest country of the world ? • How did banks start ? • Why are fireworks colourful ? • What are the Olympic Games ? • What are antibiotics ? • What is marble ? • How do we get petrol? • When did national anthems originate ? • How is silk produced ? • When did motor races start ? • What is uranium ? • What is Interpol ? • What is water ? • What are the constituents of milk ? • Where is Mona Lisa Today?

1

Why does ice float on water?

It is a matter of common experience that ice floats on water. Howsoever large the size of ice may be, it will not sink. Even icebergs which are huge masses of ice keep on floating in the sea. Do you know why ice floats on water?

The law of floatation of bodies was given by the Greek scientist Archimedes. According to this law, whenever a body is placed in water, it is acted upon by two forces—the weight of the body acting downwards and the buoyant force of water acting upwards. If the weight of the body

Only about a tenth of the ice is seen above water

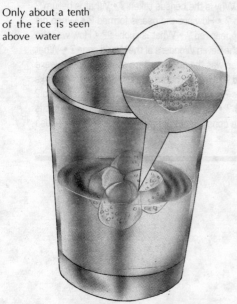

Ice floats because it is slightly lighter than water, but only about one-tenth of an iceberg can be seen above water. The rest remains hidden

is equal to or less than the upthrust of water, the body floats on water. In other words, if the weight of the body is equal to or less than the weight of the water displaced by it, it will float on water. On the other hand, if the weight of the body is more than the weight of the water displaced, the body will sink in water. Hence a body floats when its weight is equal to the weight of the water displaced. A piece of wood floats on water because its weight is less than the weight of the water displaced by it. Since the weight of wood is nearly half of the weight of an equal volume of water, half of wood is under water, while the other half is above it. Similarly, the weight of cork is nearly one-fifth of the weight of the water displaced by it, so approximately one-fifth of cork is under water while the rest remains above water. You can understand the floatation of ice also on the basis of this law.

In general, when a liquid changes to solid, it contracts because its molecules come closer to each other. As a result of this, the volume of the substance decreases or its density increases. Hence a substance becomes heavier in solid state than in the liquid state.

But water is a peculiar liquid. When it becomes ice, instead of contracting, it expands. The volume of ice becomes more than that of the water. The effect of the increase in the volume of ice is that its density becomes nine-tenth of water, that is, ice becomes lighter than water. So we get about 10 litres of ice made out of 9 litres of water. And as you know, 'litre' is a measure of volume. That is why nearly

14

nine-tenth of ice is submerged in water, while only one-tenth is above water. The ice under water (9/10 of the whole) displaces water whose weight equals that of the whole ice. This law of floatation is derived from Archimedes principle. This also explains how the maximum portion of the giant icebergs remains sub-merged in water while only a tip (1/10 part) is above water. This has been clearly shown in the diagram.

Bursting of water pipes in cold regions is due to the volume of ice being greater than that of water. As soon as water freezes, the volume is increased which produces strong force due to which pipes burst. In Finland, this property is utilised in breaking rocks. Water is filled in empty spaces available between rocks. When water freezes, it expands and generates enough pressure to cause cracks in the rocks. ○○○

2

How is dust useful to us?

It is a general belief that dust is very harmful to us. But this is only one side of the picture. Dust also is very useful to us. Before we go through the uses of dust, it is essential to know what is dust and how it is formed?

Every solid substance is composed of very small particles. When these small particles of matter are scattered, they become dust particles. For example, if we break a brick or a stone into small pieces, it will turn into small particles of dust. There are different ways by which dust is formed. When solids break, dust is formed. Smoke generated by the burning of coal, wood, petrol etc, also produces dust. Dust particles also come from dead plant and animal matter, sea salt, desert, volcanic ash etc. These particles get mixed with air

and are called dust particles. Air carries dust particles from one place to another. The particles of the earth's surface also fly in the air in the form of dust.

The biggest utility of dust particles is that they help in the formation of rains. The water-vapour in the clouds condense on dust particles in the form of water-drops. These drops fall on to the earth as rains. The absence of dust particles can delay the rain. Likewise, mist, fog etc. are also formed due to the presence of dust particles in the atmosphere.

The dust particles present in the atmosphere scatter sun-rays in all directions. Due to this scattering, there is not complete darkness for one to two hours even after the sun set. The appearance of red colour at the sunrise and the sunset is due to dust particles and water vapour. The beautiful rays of the sun seen in the twilight are also due to these dust particles. Thus we see that dust particles which are regarded as absolutely harmful by people are in reality very useful. ○○○

3

What is hypnotism?

Hypnotism is an art which can so change/control the mental state of a human being that he starts working according to the directions of the hypnotist. Man has been practising hypnotic power since ancient times to demonstrate some mysterious power, magic or miracles. A scientific study of hypnotism was started by Franz A. Mesmer, a doctor from Vienna. For a long time it was known as 'mesmerism' after the name of Mesmer. The word 'hypnotism' was used for the first time in 1840 by James Braid, a surgeon from Scotland. This word has originated from the Greek word 'hypnos' meaning 'state of sleep'.

In fact, a hypnotised person appears to be drowsing. His brain is so much influenced that he can do anything according to the directions of the hypnotist. Hypnotic power is used only over those persons who are fully willing and ready to co-operate. Nobody can be hypnotised against his wishes. The person to be hypnotised is asked to sit in a dark room. The hypnotist then repeatedly tells his subject in a very calm voice to relax and sit comfortably. Thereafter the subject is asked to concentrate his attention and focus his eyes on some object. When he gazes at that object for a long time, his eyes start getting tired. When this happens, he is asked to close his eyes. Now the subject is in a state of sleep. The hypnotist, at that moment, starts giving his suggestions and directions to him. He is now hypnotised and does everything that the hypnotist asks him to do.

Hypnotism can make a person feel as if he is blind, deaf or dumb. It can make him shiver. Hypnotism can be used to frighten people. So much so that under the influence of hypnotism a man can do things which he will never do in his normal state. When he regains his normal state, he cannot remember what he did in the hypnotised state.

Hypnotism is one of the methods of operating on patients without anaesthesia and also in dealing with mental anxieties.

Hypnosis can also be brought about by the subject himself. This is called self hypnosis or autohypnosis. Hypnosis is not a game. It can be dangerous when performed by an untrained person. ∞

Franz A. Mesmer

16

4

How is the rainbow formed?

A rainbow is an arc of multi-coloured light that appears when the sun shines through the rain.

How is the rainbow formed? Sunlight which appears to be white is actually composed of seven colours. These colours are — Violet, Indigo, Blue, Green, Yellow, Orange and Red, abbreviated as VIBGYOR, each letter of this word represents one colour. Splitting of sunlight into its constituent colours is known as dispersion and the strip of colours is known as spectrum.

Rainbow is normally seen after the rains, when the atomosphere is full of small water droplets. These spherical raindrops act like tiny prisms. As the rays of the sun fall on these, they (the rays) get refracted as they enter the raindrops, and then get reflected from the far surface of the drop. They get refracted again as they come out of the raindrops. Each component of the rays of the sun gets refracted at a different angle, thus separating out from the others. That is how we get the separation of colours.

A rainbow forms when sunlight is bent, or refracted, by raindrops

The rainbow is circular because the sun is also circular. A complete rainbow has a primary and secondary bow. The primary bow is more brilliant. Its colours are violet on the inside, then indigo, blue, green, yellow, orange and red on the outside. The colours of the dimmer secondary bow are reversed. Red is on the inside and violet is on the outside. The secondary bow is located above the primary bow. This rainbow is formed by those rays which have been reflected and refracted once again after the first reflection and refraction within the rain drops.

The rainbow is generally seen in the sky opposite the sun. It is essential for the formation of the rainbow that the sun is shining after the rain. It is also essential that the sun, our eyes and the centre of the rainbow lie on the same straight line.

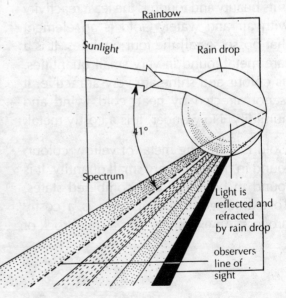

Rainbow

Sunlight

Rain drop

41°

Spectrum

Light is reflected and refracted by rain drop

observers line of sight

OOO

5

Why is gold so costly?

From the very ancient times man has a deep fascination for this shiny yellow coloured metal which symbolises affluence. The statues and temples of our gods and goddesses are decorated with gold ornaments. Kings and Emperors always gave great importance to gold. Man has always shown a great affinity for it. What is so special about gold that it has always been costly and tends to become costlier?

The increasing preciousness of a substance depends on many factors. First is its rare availability. Second factor is its utility, third is its beauty and fourth is the least reactivity with air and water. Gold is an element that possesses all the four qualities. It is a rare metal found in very small quantities. Its colour and shine are very attractive. It is not affected by heat, cold, wind and humidity. No wonder, it is a costly metal.

Gold is a shining metal of yellow colour, found in nature in very small quantity. It is found in both free and combined states. To extract gold from its ores is a costly process. An exception was a small rock of seventy and a half kilogram found in Victoria, Australia which yielded seventy kilograms of pure gold. But such rocks are rare. Extremely small quantity of gold is obtained from gold mines. It is traceable in sea water also, but its extraction from sea is uneconomical. It also occurs as fine grains is sand and gravel.

A significant portion of world's total gold production is used in ornaments. Gold is used in medicines and dentistry also. Till 1914, currencies in different countries were exchanged in terms of gold only. Even today the entire international trade is conducted with the help of gold. It is a soft and malleable metal, hence it can be easily converted into thin leaves. Thin layers of gold can be coated on other metals also. Some other metals like copper etc. are mixed in it to make it hard. It is not attacked by most acids and alkalies but dissolves in aqua regia, mixture of nitric acid and hydrochloric acid.

Gold is a means of accumulating wealth. Since the price of gold has been increasing constantly, people purchase it and hoard it instead of currency notes.

The gold mines of India are found in Karnataka. South Africa, Russia, Australia, Canada and the United States of America are the biggest producers of gold in the world. ○○○

Gold ornaments

6

Are the molecules of all substances in motion ?

Every substance is made up of very tiny particles called molecules. A molecule is the smallest part of matter that can exist independently and exhibits all the properties of that substance. For example, if we take a molecule of sugar, it will exhibit all the properties of sugar such as taste, shape, colour etc. Molecules of different substances differ in size. Some are only few billionths of a centimetre in size while some other molecules are thousand times larger. Molecules of gases are small in size. One cubic centimetre of air contains about 2.5×10^{19} (25,000, 000, 000, 000, 000, 000) molecules.

Even though a tiny piece of matter contains a very large number of molecules, there are empty spaces in between them. Molecules of matter are constantly in random motion. As the temperature increases, the motion of the molecules also increases. The hotter the substance, the faster is the motion of the molecules. Molecules of a gas move very fast in comparison to the molecules of liquids and solids. Even the molecules of ice are in motion. Isn't it surprising then that though molecules of all substances are in motion, substances don't appear shaky? Why? The reason is that there exists between the molecules a force of attraction which keeps them together. If this force is not present, the molecules of matter will scatter away in all directions.

When the molecules of a solid are heated, their speed increases and the force of attraction between them decreases. If we continue adding heat, the speed of the molecules would be still faster and the solid will change into the liquid state and, finally, to the gaseous state.   OOO

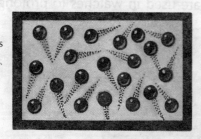

Liquid molecules are less free

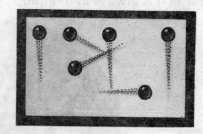

Gaseous molecules are more free

Molecules of liquid and gas in motion

7

Why do watches have jewels?

Whenever somebody purchases a wrist watch, he often enquires about the number of jewels in it. The number of jewels is inscribed or printed on the outer cases or the dial of the watch. It is commonly believed and rightly too that the larger the number of jewels, the better and more durable the watch is. Would you like to know what are jewels and why are they fitted into watches?

A good watch is one which gives correct time and does not easily go out of order. If you open a watch, you will notice that the internal mechanism of a watch is very complicated. It has many big and small parts of different kinds. A watch contains roughly 211 parts. Amongst these parts is a small wheel which is always in motion.

Along with it, there is a hair-like wire which is called a spring. When we wind the spring, the watch starts ticking. The energy stored in the spring by winding is used for running the watch. In addition to this wheel, there are many other wheels, which are constantly rotating. These wheels move the hour, minute and second hands. The axles of these wheels rest on pivots. When the wheels rotate, friction is generated between the axles and the pivots. Due to this friction, pivots and axles can wear out soon and then the watch will show incorrect time, and finally stop working. To reduce this friction, small pieces of some very hard but smooth materials are used as pivots. These small pieces are called jewels. In general, the materials to be used as jewels are ruby and sapphire. They are precious stones next to diamond in hardness. The axles of the wheels of the watches pivoted on these jewels go on rotating without experiencing much friction. Because of hardness, these jewels do not wear out soon and the watch does not go out of order easily. Hence jewels are used in watches to prolong their life.

OOO

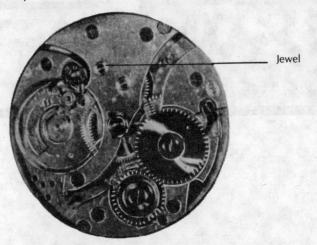

Jewel

8

How did America get its name ?

Today America is regarded as the most affluent and powerful country of the world. Its development is mainly a story of last two hundred years. Earlier it was divided into 13 small colonies. We know that America was discovered by Columbus. Then why was it not named after him? It is a matter of chance. The story as to how America was named is very interesting.

The world famous Italian traveller Columbus set out on a sea voyage in search of India. He reached some island in the morning of October 12, 1492. He landed over and named it after the name of King Ferdinand and Queen Isabella of Spain as "San Salvador". This island was just a small part of America. Now it is called the Watling Island. He misunderstood it to be India and started calling its inhabitants as Indians. Even today they are called Indians. From there he wanted to go to Japan, but, instead, he reached Cuba and Hispaniola. Disappointed with his failure to locate India, Columbus returned to Spain on March 13, 1493.

On his second voyage, which he started on September 24, 1493, he discovered several virgin islands like Puerto Rico and Jamaica. But he did not succeed in locating India. In his third journey in 1498, he discovered Trinidad and touched South America.

During this period a Spanish sailor named Amerigo Vespucci announced that he is the first person to have landed at the mainland of South America which he did on June 16, 1497. However, experts are of the opinion that Amerigo had not gone on a voyage till 1499. In 1499 Aloso de Ojeda accompanied by Florentine Amerigo Vespucci sailed up to the Orinoco straits and discovered Venezuela. During 1501–1502 Vespucci himself directed a sea voyage under the Portugese banner and discovered the shores of Brazil. It became clear to Vespucci that part of the land considered by Columbus as a portion of Asia was in fact a continent of the New World. In the beginning of the year 1500, Vespucci's writings got wide circulation and he got the credit of becoming the first European to have discovered South America. A German geographer — Waldsee Miller, named the territory of Brazil as America in honour of 'Amerigo' Vespucci. This very name caught people's attention and the entire world started using this name. ⭘⭘⭘

9

What is Red Cross and how was it born?

The Red Cross is an international humanitarian organization. Initially its field of activity was confined to looking after soldiers wounded in wars, but later it broadened its activity to alleviation of all forms of human suffering. Almost all the countries of the world have branches of Red Cross which work during both war and peace. It serves helpless people without any discrimination of caste, colour, creed or nationality. During peace time, its activities are: to give first aid, to prevent accidents, to keep drinking water safe, to train nurses and midwives, to look after maternity and child welfare centres, to establish hospitals, to set up blood banks etc. This organisation is a friend of the entire humanity.

The story of the origin of Red Cross is very interesting. The founder of this organization was Jean Henri Dunant, a Swiss Banker. On June 24, 1859, he had gone to the city of Lombardy (north Italy) in connection with his business. At that time, this city was the focal point of the continuing battle of Solferino between the French and Austrians. Thousands of men and women injured in the war were in great pain. Many of them were dying for want of first-aid. This heart-rending sight had a great impact on his mind. He forgot his own work and organised the local villagers to look after the injured of both sides in the battle. His efforts saved many lives.

In 1862, Dunant wrote a book 'A Memory of Solferino', in which he appealed to the people of the world to form special relief societies. As the soldiers wounded in war were helpless people and as human beings it was the duty of everybody to help them. This appeal had a great impact on the people and in the international conference held in Geneva in 1864, sixteen countries accepted the establishment of Red Cross. The flag of Switzerland had a white cross against red background. Changing it, a 'red cross' against a white background, was the name and flag given to this organization. Thus, Red cross came into existence. A 'Red Cross' became the emblem of this international organization that works to relieve suffering called by natural disasters, etc. and to help the victims of war.

The Red Cross has three organs. The first is the International Committee of Red Cross. It is an independent committee of twenty-five citizens of Switzerland. Its main office is situated in Geneva. The second organ is the league of the Red Cross Societies, and the third is the National Red Cross Societies.

During wars, the International Committee of Red Cross works as an intermediary between the National Red Cross societies and the countries involved in the wars. It looks after the prisoners of war in their camps and arranges relief for them. It takes care of their mail and establishes contact with their relatives. This organization also serves the people affected by cyclones, epidemics, famines etc. ○○○

10

Why was the Great Wall of China built?

We all have heard the name of the Great Wall of China. This is the longest wall of the world, being more than 2,400 kilometers (1,500 miles) long. Its height ranges from 4.57 to 9.2 metres (15 to 30 feet) while thickness is 9.75 metres (32 feet). It was built of stones and bricks. The construction of this great wall was started in the year 221 B.C. and it took almost 15 years to complete this work. Can you imagine what was the necessity of constructing such a huge wall?

This great wall was built to protect China from Mongol invaders. About the year 246 B.C., China was divided into small provinces. King Shih Huang Ti united different provinces of China into an empire. To the North of this empire lived barbaric Mongols and the king feared that they might attack his empire any time. To protect China from this danger, he ordered the construction of a huge wall. So, a wall starting from Shahi Kuan in the bay of Pohai to Chaikuman in Kansu was constructed. A road ran along the wall and signals would be sent quickly along it by patrolling soldiers.

Did the king achieve his goal? Unfortunately—no, because the wall was broken at many places and Mongols got an opportunity to attack China. The purpose of constructing the wall could never be fulfilled.

The Great wall of China is one of the very few man-made objects that is visible from the moon. ⭘⭘⭘

The great wall of China

11

What is Nobel Prize?

Nobel prizes are awarded every year for outstanding achievements in the fields of science, literature and for promoting world peace. The winners of these prizes are talked about throughout the world. Their life-sketch and works are published in the newspapers. Their names are heard on radio and television.

Sir Alfred Bernhard Nobel

Under this prize, the prize-winner gets a gold medal, a certificate and a large sum of money. The Nobel Prize is the world's most important prize. This prize is given to persons with most outstanding contributions in six fields, namely, physics, chemistry, literature, physiology or medicine, peace and economics. Economics was added in the list in 1969 for the first time. One prize is awarded in each field. If there are more than one recipients of the prize in one field, the prize money is equally distributed amongst all the winners.

Do you know how the Nobel Prize was started? It is surprisingly true that this prize was instituted by a man who was the founder inventor of the science of destruction. This scientist was Alfred Bernhard Nobel. The Nobel Prize is given after his name. He was born in Stockholm on 21st October, 1833 and he died on 10th December 1896. His father was also a scientist. Though he was a citizen of Sweden, he was educated in Russia. He invented dynamite. This material is widely used for breaking rocks, digging petrol

wells and in wars. For his valuable discovery, Nobel became famous all over the world. He earned huge sum of money from selling it. At the time of his death in 1896, he left behind a fabulous sum of 90,00,000 dollars. He left a Will indicating that the interest on this money should be given as prizes to persons for their outstanding contributions to physics, chemistry, medicine, literature and peace. This prize was named as Nobel Prize. The first Nobel Prize was given to Roentgen on 10th December 1901 for his outstanding research in X-rays. The prize money was 40,000 dollars. Even though the prize money is not large, the winners of this prize are treated with great respect all over the world.

Nobel prizes are awarded by a council called 'Nobel Foundation of Sweden'. The Royal Academy of Sciences, Stockholm, selects the best scientists of the year in the fields of physics and chemistry. The Caroline Institute of Stockholm selects the best man in the field of medical science, while the Swedish Academy of Literature does it for literature. Similarly a committee of five persons appointed by the Parliament of Norway selects the best persons for peace.

Some of the many outstanding people of the world who have received the Nobel Prize are: Albert Einstein, George Bernard Shaw, Rabindra Nath Tagore, Sir C.V. Raman, Hargobind Khorana, Mother Teressa etc.

The youngest man to receive Nobel Prize was Sir William Lawrence Bragg of England, who received the Nobel prize for physics when he was 25.

Nobel became so famous in the world that the 102nd element was named as Nobelium after him. There is an institution in Sweden which has also been named after him as Nobel Institute of Sweden.

OOO

12

How is dew formed?

You might have seen small drops of water on grass, plants and trees shining like pearls in the early hours of morning. These water-drops are called dew. Quite often people think that dew drops, like rain-water, fall on the earth from sky during night but this is not true.

Dew drops are formed due to condensation of water vapours. Air around us contains water vapours which we call moisture or humidity. Hot air contains more moisture as compared to cold air. During the night when the hot air comes into contact with some cold surface, water vapour present in it condenses on the cold surface in the form od froplets. These tiny drops of water are called dew drops. The process of dew

formation can be seen in a simple experiment. Take a tumbler and place it on a table. Now put some ice or ice-cooled water inside the tumbler. You will notice that after some time on the outer surface of the tumbler small drops of water have appeared. These water drops are formed by the condensation of the water vapours present in the air. Exactly in the same way when the trees, plants and grass become cold during night, the water vapours of the air condense on them in the form a dew.

The dew formation is more when the sky is clear and less when it is cloudy. When the sky is clear and the trees and plants, are cooler at nights, there is more evaporation of water and hence more dew formation. But when it is cloudy, trees and plants do not get cool in the night and hence there is less dew formation. As the sun rises high in the sky, these dew drops evaporate into air.

OOO

13

Why do hot things burn us?

An object is said to be hot if its temperature is more than our body temperature. If we touch such an object, heat flows from it to our body and we feel its sensation. Similarly, an object is said to be cold if its temperature is lower than our body temperature. When we touch it, heat flows from our body into that object. Do you know why it happens?

We know that our body is made up of cells. And consequently these cells are made up of molecules. At normal body temperature these molecules are in motion. When a hot substance touches a part of our body, the fast moving molecules of that substance accelerate the motion of the molecules of the cells of the affected part of our body. And when the molecules of cells of that part stand the fast vibrations, the cells start breaking up. It is the breaking up of the cells that gives the burning sensation. To repair the damaged cells, blood circulation becomes faster in the affected area. That is why the affected part becomes red.

When the temperature of the object touching the body is very high, a large number of cells and nerves break up. The heat of the substance dehydrates the cells of the skin and they break up. This is called burning.

Sometimes very hot substances destroy fat and bones. This causes deeper wounds in the body. The scars caused by such burning are removed by grafting the skin taken from other parts of the body.

Burns are classified into four degrees. In first degree burns only the superficial layers become red. In second degree burns deeper layers are damaged and blisters are formed. In third degree burns all the layers of the skin are destroyed. In fourth degree burns not only skin but tissues beneath the skin are also damaged.

Burns are not only caused by heat but also by chemicals, acids, alkalies and X-rays and radioactive rays. ⭕⭕⭕

A thing burns us when its temperature is more than that of our body

14

How is Silicon useful to us?

Silicon is a non-metallic element. It is not found in nature in a pure form. Pure Silicon is a hard, dark grey coloured material. It shines like metals and is crystalline in nature. At ordinary temperature, it does not react with other elements, but at higher temperature it makes compounds with other elements.

The earth's crust has 28% Silicon whereas china clay contains 50% Silicon. It is also found in rocks, sand, water, bones, etc. Sand has a large quantity of Silicon.

Silicon is extracted from the compound Silicon dioxide. When Silicon dioxide is heated in an electric furnace, oxygen is removed and Silicon is separated from Silicon dioxide.

Most of Silicon is found in the form of Silica which is another name of Silicon dioxide, a compound of Silicon and Oxygen. Quartz, jasper, milky stone and sand—all are different forms of Silica. Silicate is another compound of Silica. Mica and asbestos are well known forms of Silicates.

Silicates are very useful to us. They are used in making many different kinds of glasses, enamels, china clay, etc. Sodium Silicate is used in the making of soaps, prevention of the rotting of wood and eggs and in dyeing. It is also used for smoothening and for making artificial rubber.

Chief use of Silicon in its pure form is in making photocells, transistors and Silicon chips containing micro circuits for computers and other electronic components. A compound of Silicon and carbon called Silicon carbide or carborundum is used for polishing metals. By mixing Silicon in steel, its utility is enhanced. Silicon is also used for making semiconductors which have proved very useful in our life. Silicon mixed with sand and earth is used for making bricks.

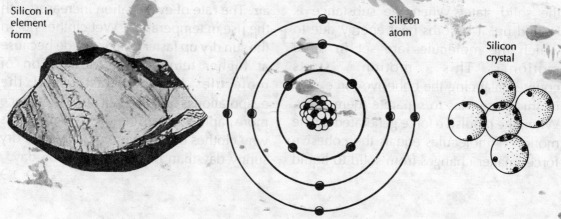

Silicon in element form

Silicon atom

Silicon crystal

Silicon is produced in the form of very pure crystals for making semiconductors

15

How is liquid converted into vapour?

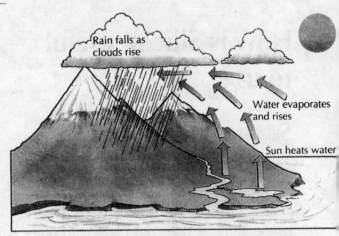

Rain falls as clouds rise

Water evaporates and rises

Sun heats water

Cloud formation

It is commonly observed during the rainy season that water falling on roads and streets disappears after a few hours. Similarly, in summer, wet clothes dry up very soon. Do you know where this water goes? This water gets converted into vapour and goes into the atmosphere. Conversion of water into vapour is called evaporation.

How does evaporation take place? Every substance is made up of very small particles called molecules. These molecules are held together by strong forces of attraction called cohesive forces. These forces are opposed by the repulsive forces caused due to the motion of mole-cules. As long as the cohesive forces are far greater than the repulsive forces, the substance remains in the solid state. When the substance is heated up, it absorbs heat energy due to which the molecules are set in rapid motion. This motion starts counterbalancing the cohesive force, that is, this force tries to separate them apart. When the repulsive force generated by the motion of molecules equals the cohesive force, matter changes from solid to liquid state. If the liquid is continued to be heated, the molecules move still faster and when the force due to the increased motion exceeds the cohesive force, the molecules of the liquid become free and escape into the air. This is how liquid is converted into vapour. The liberation of the molecules from the liquid surface into the air is called evaporation. Evaporation takes place at all temperatures.

This explains the drying up of clothes in air. The rate of evaporation increases with the rise in temperature. Wet clothes put in the sun dry up faster than in shade because at higher temperature the motion of molecules becomes faster and the evaporation is also faster. It also takes place more rapidly when the air is dry. That is why clothes dry up more quickly on a dry sunny day than on a damp cloudy day.

○○○

16

How is oxygen useful to us?

Sea-divers take oxygen cylinders with them to breathe while in the sea

Without oxygen there would have been no life on this earth. Without it no living being — trees, plants or animals can survive. Hence it will not be a misnomer to call it a life-giver. Do you know what is it and why is it absolutely essential for us?

Oxygen is a gaseous element. This was discovered by two scientists independently. Carl Scheele, a Swedish chemist, discovered oxygen in 1772 and Joseph Priestley, discovered it in 1774 in England. It is a colourless, tasteless and odourless gas. In the atmosphere the air contains 21% oxygen, 78% nitrogen and rest one percent other gases. In the earth's crust, it is found in the form of oxides of metals, the proportion being up to 50%. At—182.9°C under right pressure it can be liquefied. In the liquid state its colour becomes light blue. At—218.4°C, it can be converted into solid state.

In the laboratory, this is obtained by heating the mixture of potassium chlorate and manganese dioxide. From the atmosphere, it is obtained by the fractional distillation of air. The air is compressed to two hundred times the normal atmospheric pressure and passed through a narrow hole into a chamber. As the pressure is suddenly dropped, the air is liquefied and collected in the chamber. The nitrogen gas is separated from this by a special method and oxygen is obtained in the liquid state.

All living beings need oxygen for breathing. Plants also 'breathe' oxygen. They absorb oxygen during the night. During the day they give off oxygen by photosynthesis.

By burning oxygen gas along with the acetylene gas, a high temperature flame is produced. This flame is used for welding and cutting metals. Liquid oxygen is also used as a fuel in space vehicles.

Oxygen cylinders are used by patients having breathing difficulty and also by mountaineers and divers in the sea. This helps in the oxidation of food in our body which ultimately gives us energy. Our fuel burns due to oxygen.

We cannot breathe in pure oxygen as pure oxygen is harmful for our body cells. Fresh air is essential for us because it contains oxygen and other gases in proper proportion, therefore breathing in fresh air makes us feel fresh and active. Therefore, we should keep the doors and windows of our rooms open for fresh air. We should not cover our face while sleeping as it stops fresh air from reaching in.

We feel suffocated amidst big crowds because the quantity of oxygen becomes less there. During winter, one should not sleep in a closed room where coal is burnt to give heat. The burning of coal converts oxygen into carbon dioxide and carbon monoxide. Carbon monoxide is a poisonous gas and very injurious to health.   OOO

17

Why is the Census taken ?

Census operation is now common in almost all the countries of the world. Nothing can be definitely said as to how and when it was started. But it seems that man realised the importance of census when he started living in larger groups. It is said that the population of the world was 85 million in the year 4000 B.C. It is evident from this fact that the system of census was very much developed at that time also. Why is the census taken? The reasons for this have been different at different times. In ancient times, the king used to have census with a view to assess the number of people fit for fighting in wars. Another purpose for having census was collection of revenue. Previously, there were probably these two main reasons for conducting census, but now it has acquired greater importance.

Census helps in presenting a clear picture of different aspects of population. This helps government in the preparation and execution of plans relating to education, health, employment etc. Census tells whether the population is increasing or decreasing. The knowledge of rate of birth helps in the formation of plans to cater to the needs of people in future. It also gives the ratio of urban to rural population and is helpful in holding elections because on the basis of population only, the number of voters is fixed in a constituency or polling station. Besides, census helps in improving the law and order, economic, social and other conditions too.

The first census in our country was conducted in 1872. Since then it has been repeated every ten years. The latest census was done in the year 1992.   OOO

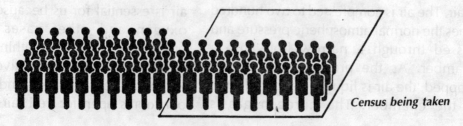

Census being taken

18

What is helium?

Most of the gases can be prepared in the laboratory but there are some which are found in nature only. Helium is one such gas.

It is an inert gas. It is odourless and tasteless. Helium has some special characteristics due to which it has proved very useful for us. It is second lightest gas next to hydrogen but it has a speciality that, unlike hydrogen, it is non inflammable.

This gas was discovered in 1868 independently by English scientists Sir Joseph Norman Lockyer and French Chemist, Pierre Janssen. While studying the solar spectrum to find the elements present in the sun, they came across some lines which were not observed earlier. These lines suggested the presence of a new element in the sun. The element was named as Helium after the Greek word 'helios' meaning 'the sun'. Thereafter, scientists made efforts to know if helium was present in the earth's atmosphere. They detected very small quantities of helium in the atmosphere. Atmospheric air contains only one part in 1,86, 000 parts, i.e., 0.0005239 percent.

On account of its lightness and non-inflammability, it is used in weather balloons. Helium is also used to ease the breathing difficulties of asthmatic patients. Deep sea divers are given a mixture of oxygen and helium for breathing so that after coming back, they do not suffer with bends. Helium is also used to weld aluminium. A mixture of helium and neon is used to produce laser beams. Helium can be liquefied at −268.9 degree centigrade. Liquid helium is used in low temperature work.

There are some places in America like Texas, New Mexico, Kansas etc. where the amount of helium present in the atmosphere goes upto 8%. It is also present in atmosphere in Canada, Africa and the Sahara desert. America is the world's richest source of this gas and is therefore the biggest seller of helium to other countries. In earlier times this gas was very costly, but now it has become quite cheaper. ○○○

Helium filled weather balloon

19

How is copper useful to us ?

Copper is a reddish orange metal that has been used for more than 5000 years. After gold it was the first metal to be discovered by man. Native copper is found in small quantities in solid or granular form. Most of it occurs in the combined state as sulphides, carbonates, silicates and oxides. Copper pyrite is its most important ore. About 50% of world's supply of copper comes from copper pyrite.

History reveals that copper was used by man as early as the Stone Age. By 4000 B.C. mining of copper had begun, by 6000 B.C. man had started using instruments, weapons and ornaments of copper. Later, man came to know that bronze, an alloy of Cu, Zn and Sn is harder than Cu. He then used bronze for making utensils, weapons and ornaments. Other alloys of copper like brass are also used for the same purposes. Copper also makes an alloy with aluminium which is called aluminium bronze. As time passed copper came to be one of the most important metals in the world, used extensively in electrical and other industries for making wires, dynamo, coils, motor coils, for minting purposes, to make coins, in engineering industry and so on. Copper is used all over the world for making electric wires because of its softness and tenacity. It is a very good conductor of electricity and heat. Much of the world's copper comes from Canada, USA, Chile, Zambia and Russia.

The process of making copper from copper ore

20

How do we get Wool from Sheep?

Warm clothes that we wear during the winter are mostly made of wool which comes from sheep. Wool is also obtained from goats and other animals like llama and alpaca. Mostly it is the wool from sheep that we use for our winter dresses. Wool is basically fine soft hair that form the coats of these above mentioned animals. Hair grow on the body of sheep, as they grow on our heads. Sheep and similar other animals have fine thick wool hair which are called fleece. The fleece or hair of a sheep insulates it from the cold in winter. In other words, wool is animal fibre forming the protective covering or fleece of sheep. Do you know how this wool comes to you from sheep? Wool is mainly obtained by shearing fleece from living animals and sometimes from slaughtered sheep also.

When the fleece is sheared, it is rolled up in bundles sorted out into different qualities or grades, cleaned, stains of various type, dried, entangled fibres are disentangled, twisted and spun in soft, loose irregular thread or yarn. Such strands used together are called 2-ply, 3-ply etc., according to the coarseness or fineness of fabric desired. Wool may be dyed at the various stages of the manufacturing process. Wool fibre is warmer but coarser than cotton, linen, silk and rayon.

Nobody knows when man first tamed the sheep. But records reveal that the primitive man had domesticated sheep both for wool and meat. After the passage of centuries, man has been able to breed many varieties of the sheep. Some of them are valuable for their wool and others for their meat. A species of sheep named 'Merino', found in Spain and Africa is highly productive in wools. Its whole body except legs and nose is covered with hair. Merino sheep are found in the United States of America and Australia also, which produce large quantities of superior wool. Wool obtained form Merino sheep is very warm.

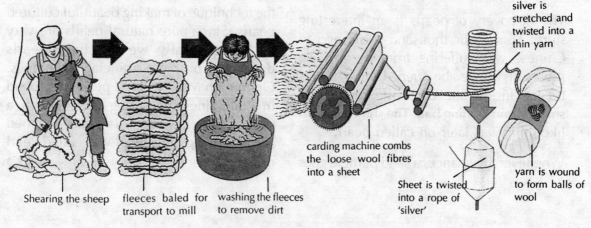

Shearing the sheep

fleeces baled for transport to mill

washing the fleeces to remove dirt

carding machine combs the loose wool fibres into a sheet

Sheet is twisted into a rope of 'silver'

silver is stretched and twisted into a thin yarn

yarn is wound to form balls of wool

The process of getting wool

Australia is the biggest producer of wool in the world. Thirty percent of world's wool is obtained from Australia alone. The United States of America ranks next to Australia. Australia's yearly production of wool is about 1700 million pounds and U.S.A. produces about 300 million pounds of wool annually. ⭕⭕⭕

21

How are the Pearls formed ?

Pure pearls are very precious. You will be surprised to know that only a small sea-creature, oyster makes them. An oyster can crawl on the ground also. The biggest tragedy with this little creature is that fish of the sea or the bigger members of its own family eat it away. When the oyster comes to the sea-shore to save its life, man eats it. In order to protect itself, it forms a hard shell around its body with a unique substance called 'nacre' or mother of Pearl. Pearls are made within this hard cover.

The discovery of pearls is an interesting story. Some four thousand years ago, a Chinese was suffering from hunger. To satiate his hunger he opened some oysters to eat. Inside one oyster he found one small round shining ball. The shinning ball-like thing was later on called pearl.

Whenever, by chance, a sand particle goes inside the shell of an oyster and rubs against the animals tender body in order to soothe this irritation, it starts depositing layers upon layers of the shell material on this particle. These layers are made up of calcium carbonate. After sometime the formation of the pearl inside the shell is completed. The pearl so formed is round, white and shining. This is called pure pearl. However, the pearls are not essentially white only. Their colours may be black, white, rose, pale blue, yellow, green, mauve also.

Man has now developed some techniques of making artificial pearls. Under these techniques sand particles are introduced inside the shell. After two or three years, when the shell is taken out of water, a pearl is found inside it. These pearls are called cultured pearls. Japan has perfected the technique of making beautiful cultured pearls. Since pure natural pearls are very costly, generally we purchase pearls developed by these artificial techniques. On the 7th May, 1934, a pearl was found in Philippines measuring 23 cm with a diameter of 13 cm. This pearl weighed about 6.37 kg. This pearl was called Pearl of Laozi. ⭕⭕⭕

22

When did the Postal System start?

We are all familiar with the importance of the postal system. It is because of this that we are able to receive letters written by our friends and relatives from England or America in six to seven days. Similarly it takes only 2-3 days for the letters to reach us from cities like Bombay, Calcutta, etc. All this is the marvel of the postal system. Mail-vans, trains and aeroplanes carry letters and messages. Millions of people are engaged in carrying postal articles including letters, packets, parcels from one place to another.

One hears stories of ancient times about messages being carried by birds and domestic animals even to far off places. Kings had royal messengers of their own who carried messages on horse back, stage coach or whatever means could be available. However, it was not possible for the common citizen to send messages. Some sort of a postal system was needed for the common man. It is said that postal system in some form or the other was present in ancient Egypt, China, Persia. It is said that the Roman Empire had the 'cursus publicus', the most highly developed postal system of the ancient world.

Around 1500 England had a post office and by 1700 England had a GPO with a Postmaster General as its head. By 1839 govt. took over the system. By 1830 there were thousands of post offices in USA. The first dispatch of mail took place between Manchester and Liverpool. In general, either the sender or the receiver paid money for the letters, the amount depending on the weight and the distance. However, the idea of postal stamps was of Sir Rowland Hill of England who introduced the postal stamp which was to be stuck on the letter by the sender. He

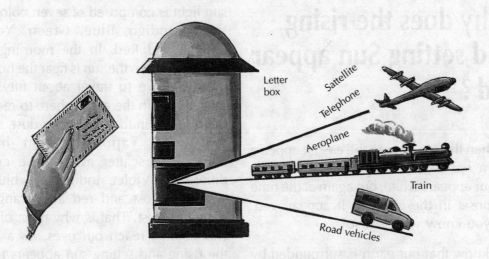

Letter box
Sattellite
Telephone
Aeroplane
Train
Road vehicles

The travel of a letter from the sender to the receiver

introduced the uniform 'penny post' for the first time in 1840. This rate was a uniform rate irrespective of the distance. It was a big step forward as it was within the common man's reach. This postal system of British spread far and wide all over the world.

Other countries of the world followed the English system and thus the postal system was established throughout the world. America has a postal system of about 7.5 lac of employees and about 1,00,000 million letters are handled by the system every year. The Air Mail service was started on the 10th of February 1911 between Hendon and Windsor in England.

The postal system of India is considered better than that of America as far as facilities are concerned. The earliest efficient postal system in India was in the 14th century which came to its height during the 16th century under the great Mughal emperor Akbar. This was a courier system. In 1837 the Imperial Post was established for an efficient postal communication. In 1854 the present Indian Postal system was established and a uniform postage rate was introduced, a step of great significance in so vast a country. In 1876 India became a member of the Universal Postal Union. A regular travelling post office service was introduced in 1870 and the railway mail service still continues to carry mail despite the development of our postal service.

More traditional forms of transport the foot runner, horse, mule, camel, bullock cart and bicycle still help distribute mail to many villages of our country through daily as well as weekly deliveries.   OOO

23

Why does the rising and setting Sun appear red ?

When the sun rises in the east, it appears like a red ball. As the day advances, its colour appears white, but again at the time of sunset in the evening, it appears red. Do you know why is it so?

We know that our earth is surrounded by the blanket of air called atmosphere. Sunlight passes through the atmosphere before it reaches us. We also know that sun light is composed of seven colours — Violet, Indigo, Blue, Green, Yellow, Orange and Red. In the mornings and evenings, when the sun is near the horizon, the rays have to travel about fifty times longer path in the atmosphere to reach us than it does in the noon. The dust, smoke and water vapour present in the atmosphere scatter away these colours differently. Violet, indigo and blue are scattered most and red and orange are scattered least. That is why most of these two colours reach our eyes. As a result, the rising and setting sun appears red.
    OOO

24

What is rubber ?

Rubber is indispensable in modern life. It being a highly elastic organic material, can be stretched eight times to its original length. It has innumerable used in houses, industries, hospitals and in farms and play things. The history of rubber is probably as old as that of nature. Three million years old fossils of the rubber producing plants have been found.

Rubber is obtained from special plants. In fact, there are more than four hundred kinds of plants and all form the juice in different quantity, of which rubber is made. The plant which gives the highest yield is called 'Hevea-Brasiliensis'. It is approximately thirty-five metres high. Another highyielding plant is Castilla.

The rubber tree originally grew in Brazil. But in the late 1800, an Englishman managed to snuggle some seedlings which were cultivated in London's Kew Garden and some in Ceylon. World's biggest supplies of natural rubber now, is Malaya.

Rubber is made of a white liquid latex which is obtained from the tree by "tapping". Latex seeps out through spiral cuts made in the bark of the tree. It, then, is made solid (coagulated), dried and exported as sheets of raw rubber. You will be surprised to know that this is a weak, sticky and not very elastic material. Its strength and elasticity are improved by the addition of sulphur in a process known as vulcanization or curing of rubber. The strength and wear-resistance of rubber are also improved by the addition of carbon black, silica and cotton flock. Natural rubber, vulcanized and filled is a widely used elastic-material. But it is rather expensive to produce.

The first useful synthetic or artificially made rubbers were produced during the World War II. Synthetic rubbers are used in industries as they are resistant to chemicals. Silicon rubbers are a fairly recent development. Their molecules of silicon atoms unlike those of carbon in others, make it resistant to the extreme heat and cold and, therefore, they are widely used as seals for jet engines.

Since the mid 1960, the production of petroleum based synthetic rubber has far outstripped the production of natural rubber.

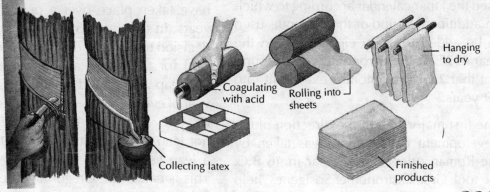

Collecting latex · Coagulating with acid · Rolling into sheets · Hanging to dry · Finished products

Processing of Rubber

25

How was the Calendar started?

In the beginning of civilization, when man observed the sun rising and setting, he felt the occurrence of the day and night. The idea of the month might have occured to him with the observation of the phases of the moon. And probably the change in the seasons gave birth to the idea of the year and the beginning of a calendar. Finally, with the development of science, man came to know things more correctly. He defined the period of revolution of the earth round the sun as one year. The time taken by the moon in completing one revolution round the earth was called a month and the time taken by the earth to complete one rotation on its axis was called a day.

In the initial calendars of Egypt, one year used to have 12 months, with one month having 30 days. The extra days were added to the year in the end to make it exactly equal to 365 days. The people of Greece used the lunar calendar according to which an additional period or three months used to be added to every eighth year. In the year 432 B.C. the astronomer Meton found out that 235 lunar months exactly fit into 19 years.

The first major step in the direction of the development of calendars was taken by the Roman ruler Julius Caesar in 46 B.C. He took Greek astronomer Sosigenes' help in this work. This calendar was based on the time taken by the earth in completing one revolution round the sun. This was named as the solar calendar. The earth completes one revolution round the sun in $365\frac{1}{4}$ days, hence this period was taken as one year. The extra quarter of a day caused confusion, so Caeser ordered that the year 46 B.C. should have 445 days to catch up. The astronomers of Caesar defined a year as consisting of 365 days and every fourth year consisted of 366 days so that one-fourth of a day left out every year was compensated in the fourth year. This fourth year was called the 'leap year'. Any year divisible by the number 4 was taken to be a leap year. 365 days of a year were divided into twelve months. The months January, March, May, July, August, October and December consisted of 31 days each, while April, June, September and November consisted of 30 days each. The month February was taken to consist of 28 days, whereas, in the leap year, it would have 29 days. This calendar continued for 1600 years. However, later on, a mistake of 10 days was detected in these calculations, because the earth actually takes 365.2422 days to complete one revolution of the sun. As such, it was natural that a difference of 7.8 days should have taken place over a period of 1000 years. In the year 1582, Gregory made a decision to drop ten days of the year 1582. And for the future accuracy he ordered that leap year should be skipped in the last year of every century unless it was divisible by 400. So 1700, 1800 and 1900 were not leap years, but the year 2000 will be a leap year having February of 29 days. This is called the Gregorian calendar and is in use all over the world.

The second calendar in use is the lunar calendar which is based on the movement of the moon. Since the moon takes $29\frac{1}{2}$ days to complete one revolution of the earth, it takes 354 days ($29\frac{1}{2} \times 12$) for twelve such revolutions. As such the lunar year, consisting of 354 days, is less than the solar year by 11 days. This way a difference of 33 days occurs in every three years. This difference is removed by making every third lunar year consisting of 13 months. This additional one month is called 'Malmas' in Hindi. To make up for the days of the month, the actual numbering of the lunar days is advanced or deferred for the necessary adjustment. On 22nd March, 1957, the Government of India introduced the Shaka calendar based on the lunar system as the official calendar. The Shaka era is behind the Christian era by 78 years.

In addition to these two calendars, some countries have other kinds of calendars also, which are used for the religious purposes of those countries.

You have already read while making the calendar, the 365 days of a year were divided into 12 months. These months have been named as January, February, March, April, May, June, July, August, September, October, November and December. Do you know how they got these names?

January is the first month of the year. It's name originated from Janus' the name of a Roman god. The Romans think that this god has two faces—one for seeing into the past and the other into the future.

February is named after the Roman festival Februo.

Mars was the warrior god of the Romans. March is named after him.

April is probably derived from the Latin word aperire which means 'to open'. Since the spring season falls in this month and there is blossoming in trees and plants, this month has been named April.

The word May is derived from the Roman goddess Maia's name.

The origin of June is not definitely known but probably this has been derived from the name of Juno—the Queen of heavens.

July is named after Julius Caesar, who was born in this month. He was the first man who made big contributions to the development of the modern calendar.

August is named after king Augustus of Rome who had won many battles in this month.

September finds its origin in the Latin word 'Septem' meaning 'seventh'. This was the seventh month in the old Roman calendar.

October comes out of the Roman word 'octo' meaning eight. In the old Roman calendar this was the eighth month.

November originates from the Latin word 'Novem', meaning nine. This was the ninth month in the old Roman calendar.

December is derived from the Latin word 'Decem', meaning tenth. This was the tenth month in the old Roman calendar. ○○○

26

How did arithmetic originate?

Arithmetic is the study of the addition, subtraction, multiplication and division of numbers. The word 'arithmetic' is derived from the Greek word 'arithmos' which means numbers. In the beginning of civilization, man used to count his sheep, cows, oxen and other animals on fingers. In fact, the word 'digit' which is used to denote numbers from zero to nine, finds its origin in the Latin word 'digitus' meaning a finger or toe. Later on, man started counting by putting marks on sticks of wood. But this process ended soon and man started using various signs for each number.

The Egyptians used straight lines for counting one to ten. The Greeks used the letters of their alphabets for this purpose. Just to make the difference clearer, a small sign used to be affixed to the letters. For example, they would write a' for one, b' for two and j' for ten. The Romans used to write the first five digits as I,II, III, IV and V. They used to write X for ten, L for fifty, C for hundred, D for five hundred and M for one thousand. In the Roman language even today numbers are written like this.

The numerals presently in use, are called Arabic numerals, because it was from the Arabs that these numerals spread to Europe. Actually, they are Indian by origin and should rightly be called Indian numerals. Zero too is Indian by origin and is called 'Shoonya', meaning 'empty' or 'nothing', which became 'sifr' in Arabic, meaning the same. In 1202 an Italian resident prepared the first book of arithmetic based on the Arabic system. The first book on arithmetic in the Latin language was printed in 1478. By that time, the arithmetical methods of addition, subtraction, multiplication and division had fully developed. Mathematicians took centuries to develop the methods now used in arithmetic. Every one who goes to school learns arithmetic. It is a skill necessary in science, business and every day life.

OOO

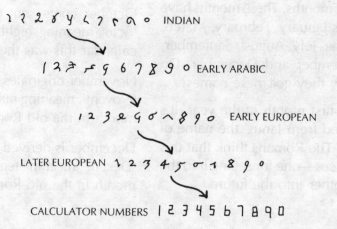

How the Indian numerals changed as they spread to Europe.

INDIAN

EARLY ARABIC

EARLY EUROPEAN

LATER EUROPEAN

CALCULATOR NUMBERS

27

Where have the Seven Wonders of the World gone ?

We have often heard about the Seven great Wonders of the ancient world. These are in fact the famous achievments of mankind in early civilizations, which the ancient Greeks and Romans regarded as the most wonderful. Would you like to know what are these Seven Wonders? They are: The Pyramids of Egypt, The Hanging Gardens of Babylon, The Tomb of Mausoleum, The Temple of Artemes, The Colossus of Rhodes of Helios, The Statue of God Zeus and The Light House of Pharos near Alexandria. Out of these seven wonders, only the Pyramids of Egypt exist and are preserved. The story behind their construction is very interesting.

The only preserved wonder—"The Pyramids of Egypt" were made some 5,000 years ago. In fact, these are the tombs of the Egyptian rulers. The biggest Pyramid is located at Giza, a small town near Cairo. This is the tomb of Pharaoh Cheops and his queen. Its area is 5 hectares. Its base forms a square and its height is approximately around 147m. 2,300,000 block of lime stone are fitted in this tomb. It is said that it was completed by more

*The seven wonders of the world: 1. **The pyramids of Egypt**, 2. **The Hanging Gardens of Babylon**, 3. **The Temple of Artemes** , 4. **The Colossus of Rhodes of Helios**, 5. **The Statue of God Zeus**, 6. **The Tomb of Mausoleum**, 7. **The Light House of Pharos***

than one lakh labourers who worked for about 20 years.

The second wonder was "The Hanging Gardens of Babylon". Around 9th century B.C. King Nebuchadnezzar had the gardens built for his wife Amytis. They were built with a series of terraces one on the top of another and 7.6 m thick walls were placed. Each terrace had enough soil depth to grow trees. The gardens were high and irrigation was done by pumping water from River Euphrates through a hidden network of pipes. In 539 B.C. Persions took control of Babylon and by 200 A.D. the people left the city in ruins.

The third wonder was the "Tomb of Mausoleum", the ruler of Halicarnassus King Mausolus wanted to build a tomb, but he died before its completion so his wife Artemisia completed the construction. The approximate height of this tomb was 42.6 m and it had a statue on its top of the King and Queen riding a horse driven Chariot. It stood for centuries, but eventually fell into ruins. An Englishman brought the Chariot's wheel and fragments of the statue which are on display in British Museum, London.

The fourth wonder of the world was "The Temple of Artemes" at Ephesus with its roof resting on too rows of 20m tall massive column. This temple was constructed in the year 550 B.C., in honour of goddess, decorated with precious stones and metals. It was burnt by a mad man in 365 B.C. Alexander the Great when conquered Ephesus decided to rebuilt this temple and by 250 B.C. it restored its original splendour.

The fifth wonder of the world was a bronze statue "The Colossus of Rhodes of Helios". Approximately 37 metres high, this was located at Rhodes island. This was constructed in the year 304 B.C. but 66 years after its construction, this statue was destroyed in an earthquake.

The sixth wonder of the world was "the statue of God Zeus" situated at Olympia. This was made by the famous sculptor Phidias in the year 433 B.C. The hair and beard of this 12 metres high statue were made of gold. Its body was made of ivory and the eyes of precious diamonds. In 394 A.D., it was taken to Constantinople where eventually it was destroyed by fire.

The seventh wonder of the world was the famous "Light House of Pharos", a peninsula near Alexandria, Egypt. The tower of white marble was completed about 279 B.C., and was about 122 metres high with a ramp leading to the top where a beacon was kept during day and night. It remained standing until A.D. 796.

OOO

28

What is echo?

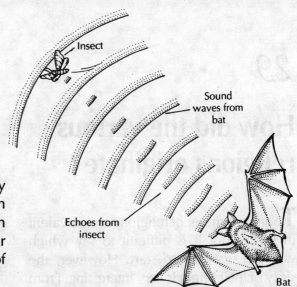

When we speak loudly in a big empty hall or in a temple, we hear our own sound repeatedly. This is called echo. An echo can also be heard by shouting near a deep ditch or a well. The thunder of clouds is another example of echo.

We know that sound travels from one place to another in the form of waves. The velocity of sound in the air is 340 metres per second.When we speak, the sound waves emanating from our mouth spread out in all the directions. When these waves meet a wall or some other obstacle in their way, they are reflected back. These reflected waves are heard by us as an echo. Hence echo is produced when sound waves are reflected by some obstacle. But all objects do not reflect sound. There are some objects like wood, jute, cardboard etc. which absorb sound.

To hear an echo, it is essential that the obstacle reflecting the sound waves must be situated at least at a distance of more than 17 metres from us. This is because the effect of sound persists on our ears for one-tenth of a second. If one sound signal has reached the ears and within one tenth of a second another sound signal reaches our ears, it will not be distinguished because during this period the effect of the earlier sound is persisting in the ear. Sound travels about 34 metres in one-tenth of a second. As such, if the object reflecting

Bats make high-pitched sounds while flying, which bounce off objects in the form of echoes. This gives the bats information about the distance and direction of the objects

the sound waves is situated 17 metres away from the speaker, the time taken for the sound to travel this distance from the speaker's mouth to the object and back to him would be one-tenth of a second and the reflected sound can be distinguished by our ear as an echo.

In Modern buildings architects use methods and materials which reduce echoes and favour good sound transmission. Auditoriums are built with rounded corners and few large flat surfaces. This prevents sound-waves from being reflected to any one position. They are scattered in many directions and the only sounds heard are those sent out from the source. Some fibre-boards having many holes are used for making rooms sound-proof. By the use of these materials the sound-waves are either absorbed or scattered so that production of echo is reduced. Radars and sonars work on the principle of echo.

ooo

29

How did the various religions originate?

Symbols of world religions: 1. Hindu God, 2. Jewish manorah, 3. Christian Cross, 4. Shinto Temple, 5. Islamic crescent moon, 6. Buddha

Today a number of religions are prevalent in the world. It is difficult to say which was the first one to start. However, the story of their origin is very interesting. From the beginning of civilization man had been worshipping many powers that could protect him from different threats in day-to-day life. For this purpose, he selected some powerful or ideal objects for worshipping. A particular spiritual power or ideal was first called a 'sect' and later on a 'religion'. Now the question is how the various major religions of the world originated?

Hinduism is not a codified religion and its origin cannot be attributed to any one person or deity. It is basically a way of life coming down from the original Aryan settlers in the Indus Valley. Buddhism started around 2500 years ago as a result of Gautam Buddha's teachings.

The principal religions in the world today are Hinduism, Buddhism, Confucianism, Taoism, Shinto, Islam, Judaism and Christianity.There are more than 300 million followers of these major religions. They constitute three-fourth of the world's total population. Approximate number of the followers of different religions is as follows: Christianity 1000 million;

Hinduism 520 million; Buddhism 230 million. Confucianism 275 million; Taoism 30 million; Shinto 36 million; Islam 520 million; Judaism 15 million.

Confucianism was founded by the followers of Saint Confucius. The Tao religion originated from the book — Tao te Ching written by Lao-tzu in the sixth century B.C. The Shinto religion is the ancient religion of Japan. Similarly, the Muslim religion (Islam) was started by prophet Mohammed. Likewise all other religions were started by different prophets. ⭘⭘⭘

30

Why and when was the Police system started ?

'Police' means an officially organised force which maintains law and order in a country. A police force works to restore peace in disturbed conditions and to protect lives and properties of the citizens. Police force is maintained by every country of the world. Do you know when and how police force came into existence?

In the beginning of civilization the chief of a race or tribe used to depend upon some warriors to maintain peace. During that time the chiefs or kings used soldiers as policemen. It was Caesar Augustus of Rome who organized a special contingent of police for the first time in the world around the year of Christ's birth for maintaining peace in his country. This system continued for three hundred and fifty years. This police force used to obey the orders of the king. In the seventh century, people started thinking of 'security police'. They felt the necessity of organising a police force, which, instead of obeying the orders of the king, should protect people and the law of the land. This thinking started in England and later spread to America.

The English were first to adopt the police system for their protection. In India the police system was started by the East India Company on December 7, 1792. Every important place was provided with officer-in-charge, a sub-inspector of police or station house officer alongwith an assistant sub-inspector, ten policemen and a police-clerk. In 1861, the first Police Act came into force and. rules regarding the uniform, salary and service conditions of the policemen were made. Then it was decided to give the policemen a uniform consisting of a red and blue-colour turban and blue clothings and heavy boots. Subsequently, many improvements were made in the police uniform. There are police forces in every country and every state which look after the security and maintain law and order. ○○○

Police forces are needed to maintain peace, law and order in the country

45

31

How were the weekdays named?

A week, sometimes called as a 'sennight', is a period of seven days usually reckoned from midnight on Saturdays. These seven days are known by different names. But thousands of years ago the division of time was of the month only. After a long time, man felt the necessity of fixing days for marketing, trade, religious activities and rest. In the beginning, at some places, every tenth day was fixed for these activities. At some other places, one day after every seven or every five days was fixed for such activities. In Babylonia, the number seven was regarded as sacred by the ancient Babylonians and therefore every seventh day was treated as a special day. The Egyptians also adopted the seven-day system. The 4 phases (new moon, quarter moon, full moon, last-quarter) of the moon take approximately 7 days each. This fact must have given man the idea to divide time into weeks of 7 days.

The Egyptians named the seven days after the names of the sun and the five planets, and the moon. The names being Sunday, Monday, Marsday, Mercury day, Jupiter day, Venus day and Saturday. The Romans also adopted this seven-day system. The present names of the weekdays are derived from the Anglo-saxon system. The days have been named after the names of their gods. The day named after the Sun God is called 'Sunnandaeg' or Sunday. The moon's day is 'Monandaeg' or Monday. Similarly the day named after the planet Mars is called 'Tiwesdaeg' or Tuesday. Instead of Mercury's name, that of God Woden was given to Wednesday. Jupiter's day became the God Thor day 'Thordaeg' or Thursday, the day of Venus was named after the wife of God Odin, Frigg as 'Friggdaeg' or Friday and Saturn's day is 'Saeterndaeg' or Saturday. A day used to be counted as an interval between the sunrise and the sunset, but the Romans counted it from midnight to next midnight. This system is now prevalent in almost all the countries of the world. OOO

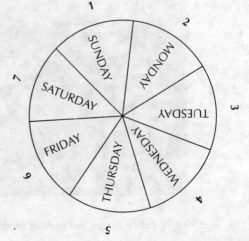

Weekdays are derived from the Anglo-saxon system.

Which is the smallest country of the world?

Country means a territory with a fixed boundary and a government of its own. Every country has its own flag and an administrative system. According to this definition, Vatican is the smallest country of the world.

Vatican is a country with the Pope, the spiritual leader of the Catholic christians, as its head. It is situated in the centre of Rome, the capital of Italy. It is fully under the control of the Pope. It has its own flag. This country has its own independent postal system, railway station, telephones and broadcasting arrangements. You will be surprised to know that the total area of this country is only 0.45 sq. kilometres. Even though this country does not have any independent source of income, it manages its affairs well from the contributions made by the catholics all over the world. In this country, the Pope's residence is a fascinating palace with a beautiful garden, a library and a museum. Vatican City maintains diplomatic relations with other countries of the world.

The story of the formation of Vatican is very interesting. For hundreds of years in the past, Italy has been the centre of activities for the Catholic Christians. For a long time, Pope had political control over a larger territory in central Italy. In 1859 this part was known as 'Papal states' and at that time its area was sixteen thousand square miles. In 1870 Rome was made the national capital of Italy and Pope's territory was merged into the Italian kingdom without his consent. As a result, relations between the King and the Pope became strained. These differences ended in 1929 with a settlement between the Italian Government and the Pope and, as a result, Vatican was recognised as an independent and sovereign state. ○○○

Vatican city

47

33

How did banks start ?

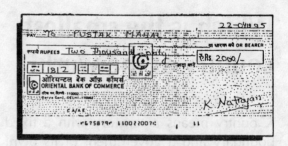

Bank Cheque

The word 'bank' is derived from the Italian word 'Banco' which means bench. In the Middle Ages, Italians used to conduct their commercial transactions while sitting on the bench. Later, this very word 'banco' underwent changes and became 'bank'. Now, all the countries of the world have banking systems. Do you know how the banks started?

Initially money lending and banking was done by the Jews and later on by goldsmiths. Merchants, in fact, paid the goldsmiths to look after their surplus cash. These goldsmiths gave receipts like a bank note to the merchants for the cash, they deposited with them. Not only that, they could lend a part of that money to others earning an interest from them. They could thus make extra money. A part of thus earned money, they gave to the merchants as an incentive to deposit money with them. This was the starting point of the savings bank or the deposit scheme in the banks at a later date.

Merchants also wrote letters to the goldsmiths to pay another merchant from their deposited money. This amounted to issue of "cheques". The modern banking system started in Venice in 1587, and in the same year the "Banco di Rialto" was established. People could deposit money in this bank and could draw when they needed it. In 1619 'Banco di Giro' took over the management of this bank. People could deposit even their gold and silver items in this bank for which the bank issued receipts. These receipts were used as currency notes.

The first bank in the U.S.A. was set up in Philadelphia in the year 1782. In England, the first bank was started in the year 1825. In India, the first bank, the Presidency Bank of Bombay, was established in 1804.

However, the first full-fledged Indian bank was the Punjab National Bank, which was started in 1894. The Government established the Reserve Bank of India in April 1935. This bank issues all the currency notes and coins for circulation in the country. Today, a large number of banks have been established in all the countries of the world.

In the beginnings, Banks had only two functions, namely to receive money and to give loans on interest. Nowadays, Banks serve many other purposes such as giving credit cards and foreign currency to people going abroad. Banks also provide us the facility of lockers to keep our valuable jewellery. ○○○

34

Why are fireworks colourful?

Fireworks (crackers etc.) are used on various occasions of national, religious and social festivals in almost all the countries of the world. It is estimated that every year a sum of Rs. 5000 crores is spent all over the world on fireworks of about 300 varieties. When they are ignited, they explode and present a riot of colours. Do you know why they are so colourful?

Fireworks are prepared by a mixture of potassium nitrate, sulphur, coal and salts of certain metals. The colour is provided by salts of metals like strontium, barium, magnesium and sodium. They are mixed with potassium chlorate. Barium salts give out green colour, while strontium sulphate produces light sky blue colour. Strontium carbonate produces yellow colour whereas strontium nitrate produces red, salts of sodium impart yellow colour, those of copper impart blue colour. Aluminium powder in the fireworks produces the silvery rain. When fireworks explode these salts burn in fireworks, various colours come out and present a spectacular sight.

The colours to fireworks are provided by salts of different metals

China was the first country to manufacture fireworks.

Hundreds of years later, Europe, Arabia and Greece also manufactured them. At present, a small town in India named Shivkashi, manufactures the largest amount of fireworks in the country.

Some time ago, in a celebration in Japan, colourful fireworks were lighted that went up to a height of 915 metres and were scattered in a radius of 305 metres. ○○○

49

35

What are the Olympic Games ?

As you know, Olympic Games are played after every four years and almost all the countries of the world participate in them. The history of Olympic Games is very old. Although much information about them is not available, it is certain that the first Olympics were played in the year 776 B.C. at a place named Olympia in southeast Greece from where they take their name. The first Olympic Games were played for five days and were witnessed by many people of Greece.

In the beginning, only the Greek players took part in these games. At that time, these games were treated as a religious festival. They were played as a mark of honour for Zeus, the chief god of the Greeks. Every player would worship at the temple of Zeus before taking part in the competition. The winner of game used to be given a branch of an olive tree which was planted in the courtyard of the temple. During those days, women did not participate in the games. So much so that they could not even see the games as spectators.

The Olympic Games continued for almost 1100 years, but in the year 393 A.D. King Theodosius of Rome, put a ban on the Olympic Games after capturing Greece. This ban continued for 1465 years. After this, in 1859, Japas of Greece organised four Olympic Games in the years 1859, 1870, 1875 and 1989. But after his death, these games were again interrupted.

A French teacher named Baron Pierre de Coubertin started the old Olympic Games once again in 1896. These games were

The Olympic symbol.

An Olympic stadium

50

played in Athens, the capital of Greece. 311 players hailing from 13 countries took part in them, 230 of them were from Greece alone.

After the first modern olympic games in 1896, they have been held in different countries every four years ever since with the exception of 1916, 1940 and 1944 because of World Wars I and II.

The Winter Olympics are also held separately in a different country. The first winter Olympics were held in 1924 at Chamon in France.

Do you know which are the games included in the Olympics? Many games are played there, amongst which the main are: football, swimming, race, wrestling, hockey, basket ball, bicycle race, shooting etc. India has been the winner of the Olympic hockey several times.

The International Olympic Committee decides as to where the next Olympic Games will be held. The Head of State of the organizing country formally declares the starting of the games. The representative of the organizing country of the previous Olympic Games hands over the Olympic flame from the temple of Zeus, then it is brought to the main stadium where the flame is kept burning till the games are over. The participating countries take part in the march-past. The Greek team is at the head and the team of the organizing country is at the tail. In between, all the participating countries take part in the march-past one after another, in order of the English alphabet. After this, the players take oath. Then white pigeons, symbols of peace, are let off and balloons are flown. On the last day, there is a valedictory function in which the Olympic flame is extinguished. ○○○

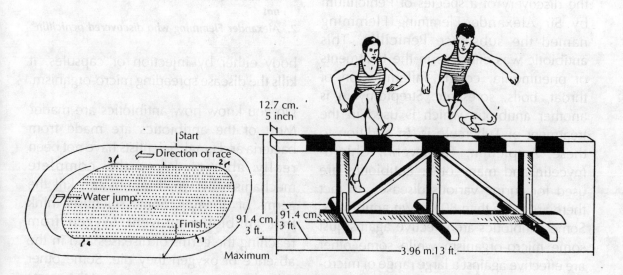

Steeple chase

51

36

What are antibiotics?

Antibiotics are special kind of medicines which inhibit the growth of or destroy bactria and some other disease producing micro-organisms. They help our body to fight against diseases hence they are used in the treatment of many diseases.

The word 'antibiotics' is derived from 'antibiosis'. 'Anti' means 'against' and 'biosis' means 'life'. Antibiotics act only against certain types of micro-organisms like bacteria. In fact, 'antibiotics' are chemical substances derived from the bodies of micro-organisms such as bacteria, moulds or some plants.

The antibiotic era began around 1928 with the discovery of a species of Penicillium by Sir Alexander Flemming. Flemming named the substance Penicillin. This antibiotic was effective in the treatments of pneumonia, cough, inflammation of throat, boils, sores etc. Streptomycin is another antibiotic which is used in the treatment of Tuberculosis. In addition to these, Ampicillin, Tetracyclin, Chloromycetin and many other antibiotics are used for curing various diseases. In fact there are more than 80 known antibiotics. Some antibiotics are effective against just some micro-organism while some other are effective against a large range of micro-organisms. Those which cover a large range are called broad-spectrum antibiotics. When an antibiotic is brought into the

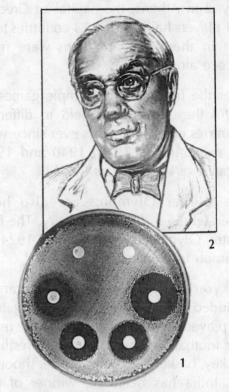

1. *This dish contains bacteria. The circles contain different antibiotics. Four antibiotics have killed the bacteria around them, but the other two have not*
2. *Alexander Flemming who discovered penicillin*

body either by injection or capsules, it kills the disease spreading micro-organism.

Do you know how antibiotics are made? Most of the antibiotics are made from bacteria and fungi. Scientists have not been really able to know the complete mechanism by which antibiotics kill the germs of diseases. Some scientists think that antibiotics prevent oxygen from reaching the germs of diseases and in the absence of oxygen they die. Some other scientists say, antibiotics prevent the germs from taking food from the body and they die for want of food. Whatever may be the mechanism of the action of antibiotics, it is an established fact that these medicines have proved very useful for mankind. Every year millions of people in the world suffering from various diseases are saved by these medicines. In 1930, 20% to 85% of total deaths in America were due to pneumonia. In 1960, this figure came down to 5%. Similarly, the deaths due to typhoid have come down from 10% to 2%. Infectious diseases can also be checked with their help. They are also useful in preventing diseases like throat infection, rheumatic fever, venereal diseases etc.

They have their adverse effects also, such as reaction of the body to them, rashes and other symptoms may develop or they may cause other diseases. An extreme reaction may even lead to death. Sometimes, they are ineffective on the germs of the diseases. ⚬⚬⚬

37

What is marble ?

Marble is a kind of lime stone which is available in many colours. White marble has been in use for construction of buildings since ancient times. The people of Greece and Egypt used this stone for construction of temples. The Taj Mahal of Agra is also made from the white marble. It is unaffected by heat, cold, rains etc.

Marble is found in nature in the form of rocks. You may not be aware as to how these rocks are formed? These rocks are formed from lime-stones.The tremendous heat and pressure beneath the earth's surface converts lime-stone into marble rocks. If you analyse the chemical composition of marble, you will find that it is mostly calcium carbonate. Some varieties of marble contain ninety-nine per cent calcium carbonate. Marble acquires a variety of colours due to the presence of some salts of aluminium and magnesium in it. Pure marble is snow white.

It is cut into big pieces from the rocks by machines. These big pieces are brought to workshop where they are cut into convenient desired sizes. Marble obtained from rocks is initially coarse. To smoothen its surface, it is polished with the help of special machines. After this it is ready for use. Italy has some of the vast and well known marble quarries in the world. About one lakh tonnes of marble is obtained in Italy every year. The longest marble quarry of USA is located in Vermont.

Because of its beauty, it has always been a favourite material for sculpture, architecture and many other purposes. Famous sculptors, like Michelangelo and Leonardo da Vinci used marble for many of their works.

In India, Bheraghat in Jabalpur (M.P.) is such a place where rocks of marble are found in abundance. Rocks of marble are also found in Rajasthan. Marble of Makrana is very famous. ⚬⚬⚬

38

How do we get petrol?

Petrol is one of the most useful products in the world. Cars, scooters, aeroplanes and various other automobiles—all consume it as their fuel. It is also the source of light and other forms of energies.

Petrol is obtained from petroleum—a viscous dark-coloured liquid found inside the earth. The word 'petroleum' is derived from the two Latin words 'petra' and 'oleum' meaning rock and oil respectively. It is found usually in pools beneath the earth's surface. Petroleum is sometimes called 'black gold' because it is highly useful for us. Do you know how this oil is formed inside the earth?

Millions of years ago, plants and animals got buried in earth's interior due to geological upheavals. Intense pressure and

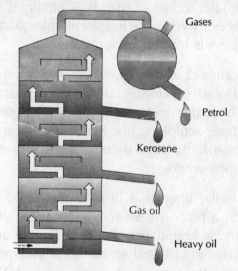

Process of fractional distillation

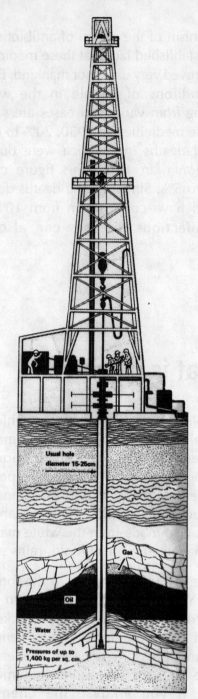

Crude oil being extracted from an oil-well

heat inside the earth converted the decomposed plants and animals into petroleum. Man discovered its massive stocks in the sea-bed too.

The crude oil is drawn out of petroleum wells. This consists of petrol, naptha, kerosene, diesel, pitch etc. It is brought to refineries for purification and extraction of these products. The crude oil is heated in very big cylindrical vessels. The various constituents of the oil are separated as different fractions at different temperatures and taken out through separate pipes. This process is known as fractional distillation. The various other products obtained from petroleum include plastics, paints, drugs, explosives, cleaning fluids and detergents.

Scientists have succeeded in synthesising petrol by some artificial techniques also but petrol prepared in this way is costlier.

It is found in many countries but mainly in Gulf countries, USA and Russia. In India, it is mainly found in Assam and Bombay. ○○○

39

When did national anthems originate?

Today every country of the world has her own national anthem. National anthems are sung or played on special occasions by almost all the countries of the world. They are patriotic songs sung as a mark of honour to the countries concerned. These are sung to inspire patriotic feelings in people.

There is no authentic record as to how and when national anthems originated. It is believed that the 'Kim Gao' song sung in Japan in the ninth century was the first national anthem of the world. 'God save the Queen' was considered as the national anthem of Britain in 1825, although it had been popular as a patriotic song and used on the occasions of royal ceremonies since the mid 18th century.

The national anthem of the United States of America was written during 1814. Francis Scott Key, an American lawyer, was aboard one of the British ships that attacked 'Fort McHenry'. All through the night, Key watched the attack. When at dawn he saw the American flag still flying over the fort, he was overwhelmed by patriotic feelings. He immediately wrote a line on an envelope which later formed part of the national anthem of America.

Japan and Jordan have the shortest national anthems in the world—each of four lines only.

Our national anthem was written by Rabindra Nath Tagore. This was sung for the first time at the Calcutta session of the All India Congress in December 1911. On 24 January 1950 'Jan Gan Man Adhinayak' was adopted as the national anthem of India. 'Vande Mataram'—a patriotic song written by Bankim Chandra Chatterjee was also given status almost similar to that of the national anthem. Today, all the countries of the world have their own national anthems. ○○○

40

How is silk produced?

All of us are familiar with the soft and beautiful clothes made of silk. Silken cloth can be made so thin that a full bale of it can be passed through a small ring. Do you know how it is made?

You may be surprised to know that silk threads are made by small insects called silkworms. A silkworm makes a cocoon around itself which increases in size as the worm grows bigger. When the cocoon becomes big, it is heated in hot water. In this process the worm dies and silk is obtained from the cocoon. If this worm is allowed to grow it turns into butterfly.

The Chinese knew the art of making silk four thousand years ago. There is an interesting story in this regard. It is said that the Chinese Queen Si Ling-Shi once put a silkworm by mistake in a water pot which was meant for washing hands. The next day she saw silk threads coming out of the pot. Fascinated by it, she started keeping silkworms and used the silk prepared by them for wearing. For years, the Chinese kept the art of making silk a secret. The Japanese were the first to know this secret in the third century. Around A.D. 550, King Justinian of Byzantium sent two Persian monks to China as spies. On their return these two spies brought eggs of the silkworms in a bamboo tube. After this, art of obtaining silk from the silkworms slowly spread throughout the world.

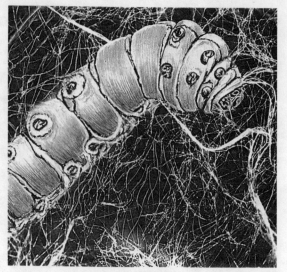
A cocoon

Today, countries like China, Japan, India, France, Spain, Russia and Italy produce silk.

In the beginning of the summer season, the female worm lays about 500 eggs on the leaves of mulberry. In around ten days, larvae come out of these eggs. They are carefully examined and the diseased ones are separated and destroyed. The silk worms are brought up on the leaves of the mulberry. Silk is made from the juice coming through a hole in the mouth of the silk worms. In about 25 days, they give out cocoons. One-fifth of the weight of a cocoon is silk. The silkworms are killed in hot water and silk is spun out. A cocoon has one long thread measuring from 500 to 1300 metres. It is almost as strong as a steel wire of the same thickness.

Silk blended with cotton as well as with other synthetic fibres too is produced and is very beautiful. For beauty and finesse, Italian silk is regarded as the best in the world today. ○○○

41

When did motor races start ?

Man has been fond of competition and races since ancient times. In the Middle Ages, he used to participate in horse and chariot races. Later, he got bicycle as an excellent vehicle for racing. Then came the development of motor cars which generated tremendous speed and thrill in such competitions.

The first motor race of the world was held at 8 a.m. on July 22, 1894. Twenty-one cars participated in this race from Paris to Rouen. But this was only an exhibition race. A real race first took place on June 11, 1895 from Paris to Bordeux, covering a distance of 1,178 km. Later, most of the races were held in circular tracks.

The oldest motor race of the world first took place on September 14, 1905. This was conducted for awarding the R.A.C. Tourist Trophy. The first inter-continental motor race was held in Sicily on May 9,1906. The Grand Prix motor race was held on June 26–27, 1906 in France.

The fastest motor race of the world was held on February 8, 1964 in the US. In this race Richard Peri of North Carolina covered a distance of 80km in 17 minutes 27 seconds, averaging a fantastic speed of 275 km per hour. Francois Lecket of France established an interesting record of covering a distance of 4,00,000 kilometres by driving for 363 days out of 370 days from the 22nd July 1935 to 26th July 1936. Eight persons of France drove a distance of 1,85,353 miles and 1741 yards in a period of 133 days, 17 hours, 37 minutes and 38.6 seconds between March to July 1933, thus averaging a speed of about 93 km per hour.

Juan Manual Fangio, born on June 24, 1911 in Argentina is known to be the most successful motor racer of the world. He had won twenty-four races by 1958 when he finally retired.

There are many advantages of participating in motor races. While participants receive instant fame around the world, they also get fabulous prize money on winning these races. The biggest advantage is reaped by the motor company whose car comes first in the race as it gets highly publicized.

A formula racing car

42

What is Uranium?

Uranium is a silvery, radio-active, metallic element. It occurs as uranium oxide in the mineral pitchblende.

Uranium was discovered by the German chemist Heinrich Martin Klaproth in the year 1789 from a mineral called pitchblende. He named it 'Uranit'. But, after a year Klaproth changed its name to Uranium after the planet Uranus. By the end of the eighteenth century scientists had already made many compounds of this metal. In 1896 Henry Becquerel discovered radioactivity in Uranium.

Uranium is a shining metal of white colour but it turns black when it comes in contact with the atmosphere. Uranium is a very heavy metal. The weight of a cubic foot of this metal is approximately half a ton. In the beginning, it was used for dyeing silk and porcelain vessels.

Natural Uranium is a mixture of two main isotopes — Uranium-238 and Uranium-235. 99.27% of the Uranium found in nature is uranium-238 and 0.72% is Uranium-235.

Two of its unique properties have enhanced its utility throughout the world. The radioactive rays coming out from the nucleus of Uranium are very useful. These rays are used in agriculture, industries, biology and medical research. The second use of Uranium is in the field of nuclear energy. In 1938 the process of nuclear fission was discovered by bombarding Uranium nucleus with neutrons. The nuclear fission is the process in which the nucleus of the Uranium-235 atom is split into two parts by neutron bombardment, hence tremendous energy is produced. The atom bombs were made through this process only in 1945 which were used against Japan in World War II. After the development of the atom bomb, its utility increased tremendously.

Nowaday nuclear fission is used for producing electrical energy. You will be surprised to note that a pound of Uranium produces as much energy as we get from the burning of three million pounds of coal. Therefore, the Uranium-235 isotopes are used in nuclear reactors for the production of energy. The energy produced in the nuclear reactor is used to heat water to make steam. This steam runs the turbines and thus electricity is produced.

Uranium is also used to absorb X-rays and gamma rays. Its oxides are used as catalysts in some chemical reactions.

There are four parts of Uranium in every one million parts of the earth's crust. The compounds of Uranium are also found in the rocks. Pitchblende is one of the important ores of Uranium. Its ores are found in abundance in England, India and Africa.   ○○○

43

What is Interpol?

The logo of Interpol

Interpol is an international criminal police organization. The word 'Interpol' is derived from the two words 'international' and 'police' and stands for the International Criminal Police Commission. Interpol is a strictly non-political, non-religious, non-racial organization in which the police forces of more than hundred different nations cooperate with each other. Its headquarters are situated in Paris.

The job of the Interpol is to trace criminals. According to international law, police of one country cannot enter the territory of another country to apprehend a criminal who, after committing a crime, has absconded there. Interpol helps in such situations to trace out the criminals. Every country has its representative in Interpol.

After the First World War, crimes increased considerably in Europe, specially in Austria. After committing crimes, criminals used to go to some neighbouring country and hide themselves there. In order to arrest such criminals, Johann Scober, the then police chief of Vienna, called a meeting of the police officials of different countries in 1923. It was in this meeting that twenty countries jointly established Interpol. Its first head office was made in Vienna and Johann became its first president.

In 1938 Germany invaded Austria and with this came the end of the Interpol. During the Second World War Interpol remained inactive. After this War, Flaurent Lovagay, Inspector General of Belgium police revived it. Due to the unavailability of ncessary facilities in Belgium, the head office of Interpol could not be established there. Paris became its new head office. By 1955, fifty-five countries became members of Interpol. India continues to be a member of Interpol since 1938. In 1956, Interpol was given a new constitution.

Interpol makes use of the most modern scientific means to catch criminals. To trace and arrest criminals is the only function of this organisation. It cannot be used for any political, military or religious activity.

ooo

44

What is Water?

Like air, water is essential for life. Without water we cannot survive for more than a few days. Human beings, trees, plants and animals all need water for their survival. Perhaps, that is why nature has covered more than seventy percent of the earth's surface with water. About 97% of water on earth is in the oceans.

Water is a compound of hydrogen and oxygen. It contains two parts of hydrogen and one part of oxygen by volume. Pure water is colourless, odourless and tasteless. We get water from rivers, lakes, fountains, wells, rains, oceans etc. Water exists in three states—solid, liquid and gaseous. Normally it is found in liquid state, but when it is cooled to zero degree centigrade, it freezes into ice. When it is heated to 100° C, it is converted into steam.

Water obtained from nature is not pure, but contains many salts and minerals dissolved in it. Due to these impurities, water develops some taste. Some of the impurities make water hard. Hard water does not form lather with soap. The hardness of water is of two types—temporary and permanent. Temporary hardness is due to the presence of bicarbonates of calcium and magnesium. It is removed by boiling the water. Permanent hardness is caused by the presence of chlorides and sulphates of calcium and magnesium. This hardness is removed by mixing sodium carbonate in water.

Water has many fascinating properties. For example, ice is lighter than water. That is why ice and big icebergs float on water. Water has the highest density at 4° C. Due to this property, during winter, only the upper surface of water in lakes and ponds freezes but the lower portions do not freeze. Hence marine life can survive in such lakes and ponds easily. The structure of water is such that most substances dissolve in it. Water is regarded as a universal solvent. Sea-water is saline because many minerals remain dissolved in it. Air dissolves itself in water enabling aquatic animals to breathe inside water. Water is a liquid which is not easily evaporated. That is why soil retains moisture for a longer period and trees and plants are, therefore, benefited by this.

Water content in different living organisms varies. Trees and plants have 60% to 80% water, fresh fruits 85% to 95% and plants living in water, contain 98% water. Human body contains 65% water.

A civilized man on an average uses 35 gallons of water every day for drinking, bathing and washing. One should be careful about ones drinking water. Often water contains germs of dangerous diseases like typhoid, cholera, diarrhoea, dysentery etc. Boiled water is, therefore, hygienic. Water can be made free from germs by filtering, boiling and mixing potassium permanganate or bleaching powder in it. ooo

45

What are the constituents of milk?

Milk is white nutritious liquid produced by female mammals as food for their young ones. Milk obtained, especially from cows, buffaloes, goats, etc. is drunk by human beings. Butter, cheese, curd, etc. are also made from it.

Nothing definite can be said as to when exactly man started using milk but it is certain that around 5000 years ago man had started domesticating milk-producing animals.

Cow, buffalo, sheep and goat are the main milk producing animals. In northern Europe, milk from reindeer is also used. In the Middle East countries, goat's milk is commonly used for consumption.

From the very beginning, milk has been known to be a perfect food. It contains all the nutritional elements like sugar, proteins, fats, vitamins, minerals, salts and water needed to our body. Cow's milk contains 87.2% water, 3.7% fat, 3.5% proteins, 4.9% sugar and many minerals and vitamins. The milk of various other animals contains all the above mentioned nutrients in varying percentages.

We extract fat present in milk in the form of butter. Fats give us extra energy. The proteins present in the milk strengthen the muscles of our body. The sugar is easily absorbed by the body and acts as a fuel. Minerals like calcium and phosphorus are useful for our bone formation. Vitamins A, B, C, D, E, K and niacin present in milk reduce the vitamin deficiency of our body.

Milk gets spoiled very soon. As such, it should be cooled to 10° C within two hours of milking. It should be maintained at this temperature till it is transported to other places. Its fermentation can be prevented by boiling it several times a day.

In many countries, pasteurized and homogenized milk is sold. Skimmed milk is popular with dieters because most of the fat is removed before the milk is sent out for sale. ○○○

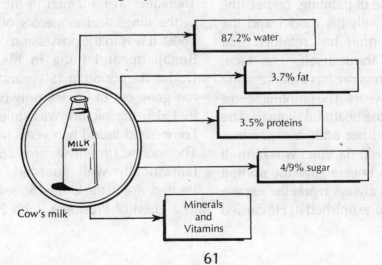

Cow's milk — 87.2% water — 3.7% fat — 3.5% proteins — 4/9% sugar — Minerals and Vitamins

46

Where is Mona Lisa Today?

Mona Lisa

Mona Lisa is one of the most famous paintings of Leonardo da Vinci. It is a picture of a woman who is smiling mysteriously. Many people have wondered what she was smiling at. Leonardo's famous painting, the Mona Lisa, today hangs in the Louvre museum Paris preserving some of the world's rarest art pieces and antiques which are beyond all evaluation today.

Mona Lisa was painted by Leonardo da Vinci between 1503 and 1506. Mona Lisa was the wife of a Florentine gentleman, Francesco del Gioconda. That is why she is also called La Gioconda. Leonardo was 51 and she was 24 when the painting started. She used to come to the great master's studio in the later afternoon when the light was soft. Leonardo worked hard on this painting for about three years. During the course of painting, he became fascinated both with his model and the portrait. The portrait has retained that exclusive aura about itself. The face, enigmatic in expression, has tantalized the millions over the years. The painting seems to be as alive as the beautiful woman. The landscape behind her adds a mysterious backdrop. Leonardo da Vinci was himself charmed by it and never gave the portrait to Francesco. He always made the excuse that he had not quite finished it. He carried it with him wherever he went. While he painted her portrait, Leonardo used musicians, singers and jesters to keep her in a merry mood.

In 1516 when Leonardo migrated to France from Italy he was given a beautiful palace in Loire Valley by King Frances I. It is believed that Francis I paid, 4000 gold crowns for the Mona Lisa but could acquire it only after the artist's death in 1519. Thereafter, it remained in the possession of the kings and emperors of France. In 1800, it was in the possession of Napoleon Bonaparte and hung in his bedroom. During the period of 450 years this portrait has gone out of France only twice. Once in 1911, the picture was stolen from the Louvre and found two years later in Italy. The second time it was for 26 days on a fantastically well guarded and highly insured visit to the United States of America as a guest of President, John F. Kennedy.

○○○

2
Science &
Technology

• How do we see clearly with spectacles? • What is dry ice? • What are the methods of time measurement?
• What is Plastic? • What are different types of telescopes? • What is Plastic Surgery? • How does a washing
machine work? • How does a dish washer work? • How is food packed in cans? • What is star Television?
• What is a cellular phone? • How are skyscrapers built? • How is synthetic rubber made? • What is an Alkaline
Battery? • What is automatic door operation? • What is the remote control of a television set? • How does a
steam iron work? • What is LPG? • What is bar code? • What is the principle of an autopilot? • What is a
Compact Disc?

1

How do we see clearly with spectacles ?

Wearing a pair of spectacles is a common sight. All men, women and children, who have weak eye-sight, use spectacles. Scientists have developed spectacles that help in seeing both the near and distant objects clearly. Nowadays, lenses are used inside the eyes in place of spectacles. These are known as contact lenses. These lenses can be of different colours and are used by those who do not want to wear spectacles.

The use of spectacles was started some 700 years ago. In 1266, Roger Bacon of England used a piece of glass to magnify the words written in a book. This glass piece was cut out of a spherical ball of glass. But it is not definitely known as to

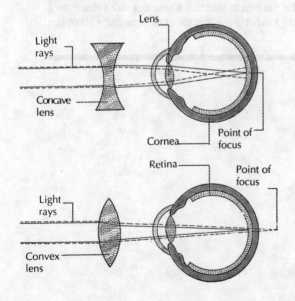

when glass pieces were used in the form of spectacles.

Spectacles are shown on the eyes of one Cardinal Ugon's portrait made in 1352. This proves that spectacles were developed during the period 1266–1352. By the sixteenth century, they were very much in use. In 1784, Benjamin Franklin brought wonders in the field of spectacles by making bifocal lenses. A question must be coming to your mind as to how do we see clearly with the help of a pair of spectacles?

It is so simple. Our eyes act as a camera. The light rays enter our eyes through cornea (black portion of the eye). There is a convex lens inside the eye, and behind this lens there is a screen which is called the retina. The light rays coming from any object make an inverted image of the object on the retina with the help of this lens. This image is carried to the brain by the optic nerve. It becomes erected there. This is how we see an object. If the eyes have no defect, the focal length of this lens gets automatically adjusted and the image of the object always falls exactly on the retina. But, sometimes, the eyes develop some defects due to which the image of the object is formed before or behind the retina. Thus, the object appears blurred. Persons having such eye-defects need the assistance of spectacles. The defects of the eyes are mainly of three types.

Myopia: Persons suffering from this defect can see the nearby objects clearly, but the distant objects appear blurred. The image of the objects due to this defect is formed before the retina. This defect is corrected by using concave lenses in the spectacles so that the image of a distant object is formed on the retina.

Hypermetropia: Persons suffering from this defect cannot see nearby objects clearly but can see distant objects clearly. Short distance objects make their images behind the retina. This defect is corrected by using convex lenses in the spectacles so that the image of the object is again formed on the retina.

Astigmatism: Due to this defect in the eyes, one cannot see with clarity the horizontal and vertical lines simultaneously. Spectacles with cylindrical lenses are used to correct this defect.

Bifocal lenses have both concave and convex lenses so that these can be used by people who are suffering from both myopia and hypermetropia.

In this way, spectacles can help man to see objects clearly. Spectacles have proved to be a great boon for persons with weak vision. In addition, to protect the eyes from the intense rays of the sun, goggles, cooling glasses (sun glasses) are used. Coloured glasses are used in these, which prevent the ultra-violet rays of the sun from entering the eyes. The ultra-violet rays are very injurious to the eyes because they can burn the tissues due to their high energy content.   OOO

2

What is dry ice ?

Ice, which we generally see around us, is made by freezing the water. Water turns into ice when it is cooled to 0°C. There is another kind of ice which is known as dry ice.

Dry ice is solid carbondioxide. It is formed when carbondioxide turns directly from a gas into a solid at a temperature of about −80°C. It is so cold that if held in hand it couses frost bite. It is usually prepared by cooling carbondioxide under high pressure. It looks rather like snow but can be made into blocks by compressing the flakes. Dry ice is very heavy.

Dry ice is very important for cooling or

Vaporized dry ice

refrigerating foods such as ice creams and meat and medicines. It is also used to stimulate fog and steam effects in television or stage plays because it rapidly turns back to gas at ordinary temperature without becoming liquid.   OOO

3

What are the methods of time measurement?

1. Sundial
2. Hour Glass
3. Water Clock
4. Atomic Clock
5. Quartz Watch
6. Pendulum Clock

Different Methods used for the measurement of time.

Through the ages, man has used many methods of time measurement such as rotation of the earth, rising and setting of the sun, movement of the moon and stars and the change of seasons. Perhaps the earliest measurement of time was based on the regular cycle of night and day. The 24 hour period between one mid night and the next was called the mean solar day.

Time measurement by the earth's rotation with respect to the sun is called sidereal time. A sidereal day lasts 23 hours, 56 minutes and 4 seconds. The time the earth takes to complete one revolution around the sun, is called the sidereal year. The sidereal year lasts 365 days, 6 hours, 9 minutes and 9.54 seconds. Sidereal time is more accurate than solar time.

The oldest methods for measuring time include sundial, candle clocks, water clocks and hour glasses. In a sun dial, time was measured by the length of the shadow of a stick casted by the sun. With candle clocks, time was measured by the rate of a burning candle. The water clock was a leaking bowl. In the hour glass, sand flowed from one container into another at a steady rate. By measuring the amount of sand in either container, a person could tell how much time had passed.

The development of clocks that worked by springs started in the late 1400. The two main types of modern clocks are — mechanical clocks and electronic clocks. Mechanical clocks are powered by various devices that must be wound while the electronic clocks are battery powered. Quartz based clocks are also battery driven. Most of the quartz clocks which are based on quartz crystal vibrations are accurate upto 60 seconds in a year.

Digital clocks and watches which became popular in the 1970s are also very accurate time measuring devices. Most of them have liquid crystal display system or light-emitting diode display system. These are also quartz based.

The most accurate means of measuring time is an atomic clock. An atomic clock measures the vibrations of certain atoms of cesium or amonia gas which keep extremely accurate time. In 1000,000 years an atomic clock may loose or gain only a few seconds. The world time changed to atomic time standard in 1972. ○○○

4

What is Plastic?

Plastics do not occur naturally but are manufactured. The word 'plastic' has originated from the Greek word 'Plastikos' which means 'to mould'. It is made from simple organic chemicals. It has many varieties and colours.

Plastic was invented by Alexander Parkes of England in 1862. In those days it was called 'Parkesine' after him. Parkesine was the first plastic ever produced.

Many plastics have 'poly' in their names for example, polythene. Poly comes from a Greek word meaning 'many'. Polythene means 'many molecules of ethene joined together'.

The manufacturing of plastic on a commercial scale was started for the first time by Leo Hendirk Backeland. He made it from phenol and formaldehyde. Subsequently, new techniques were developed for the production of plastics. Today, scientists have discovered many raw materials which are used in the making of various kinds of plastic products. Most plastics are made from chemicals found in oil, although a few come from wood, coal and natural gas. Common types include polythene, polystyrene, PVC and nylon.

Today, plastic has become an integral part of our life. Its uses are endless. Transparent plastics are used for making lenses and windows of aeroplanes. Polythene bags, a plastic product, are used in almost all walks of life. Articles of domestic use like buckets, cups, brushes, combs, baskets, cabinets for radios, transistors etc. are also made of plastics. Toys and sports goods made from plastic have flooded the markets everywhere. The yarn for making terylene cloth is, in fact, made from plastic. Today scientists have even succeeded in developing heat insulating plastics. Foam cushions, seats in trains, cars and aeroplanes—all are made from plastics. Now, plastics are used as surgical aids also. There is hardly any field of life in which plastics are not used.   ooo

Cup   Bag   Comb   Tooth Brush   Basket   Socket   Disk   Bucket   Tube   Plug   Taperecord

Various plastic-items of domestic use

5

What are different types of telescopes?

A telescope is an optical instrument used to see distant objects clearly and magnified. The telescope was invented in 1608 by a Dutch optician Hans Lippershey. In 1609, the Italian astronomer Galileo made his first telescope and observed the rings of Saturn and Jupiter's moons. Today there are three main kinds of telescopes: refracting telescopes, reflecting telescopes and radio telescopes.

Refracting Telescopes

A refracting telescope makes use of two lenses fitted at the end of a tube. An astronomical telescope consists of one larger size convex objective lens and a convex eyepiece while a Galilean telescope makes use of a convex objective lens and a concave eyepiece. Modern refracting telescopes usually contain complicated lens systems to correct chromatic aberrations.

Radio telescope.

Reflecting Telescope

A reflecting telescope is made of a concave mirror that gathers and focuses light waves. Another mirror near the point where waves come together, reflects light into the eyepiece.

A Newtonian telescope uses a mirror set at a 45° angle to reflect the light into the eyepiece. A Casegranian telescope has convex mirror which reflects light through a tiny hole in the centre of the objective mirror. The light passes through to the eyepiece, which makes the image larger.

Refracting telescope

Newton's reflecting telescope

Cassegrain reflecting telescope

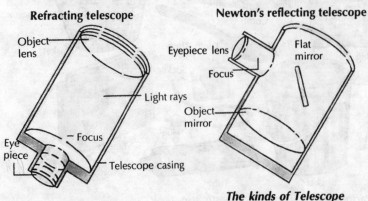
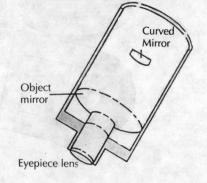

The kinds of Telescope

The largest reflecting telescope in the world is at the Yerkes observatory in Wisconsin. Its objective lens has a 102cm diameter. The palomar observatory in California has a reflecting mirror with a diameter of 508cm.

Radio Telescopes

A radio telescope has a huge reflector shaped like a bowl which reflects radiowaves to a detector. Radio telescopes are used in astronomy. These telescopes can be used under all weather conditions.

OOO

6

What is Plastic Surgery ?

Plastic surgery is a branch of surgery devoted to restoration, repair and correction of malformations of tissues. It concerns not only return to normal appearance but also the restoration of function. The field of plastic surgery has several sub-divisions such as cosmetic surgery, management of congenital defects, burns, wounds and other acquired defects.

Cosmetic surgery deals with improving the appearance of tissues or organs such as the nose, face, eyes or breasts. The most common types of cosmetic surgery are face lift to remove wrinkles from the face and neck and a rhinoplasty to change the shape of the nose.

Plastic surgeons treat physical defects that exist since birth (congenital defects) or are caused by injury or disease. Often the body part that is defective or damaged does not work as it should. In such cases, the surgeon does reconstructive plastic surgery. This often requires grafting. In grafting skin muscle, bone or cartilage is transplanted from a healthy part of the body to the hurt or damaged part. Sometimes reconstructive surgery involves reattaching several limbs, rebuilding damaged tissues, restoring damaged blood vessels and nerves. Plastic surgeons are available almost in all the hospitals.

Plastic surgery has been practised for hundreds of years in China and India. Chinese and Indian doctors were reshaping noses and lips long ago.   OOO

Plastic surgeon separates layers of skin cells for use in skin grafts..

7

How does a washing machine work?

A washing machine is an electrically operated machine used to clean dirty clothes. Most washing machines have a round drum that spins to wash the clothes. The clothes tumble over each other as it turns, which helps the detergent to clean them.

In a modern washing machine, a set of buttons allows the user to select a pre-programmed cycle of washing, rinsing and removing the water. At the start of the cycle, water pours in through an electrically controlled inlet valve. Once the water reaches a certain level in the drum, this is detected by a senser that turns off the inlet valve. The pressure of the water in the inlet pipe helps to shut the valve firmly. If required, the water is then heated by the machine's heating element. Once the preset temperature is reached, a thermostat switches off the electric supply to the heater. The dirty clothes are cleaned by the detergent mixed in water in the spinning drum. The clothes are rinsed in clean water to remove the soapy water.

The clothes may be washed and rinsed several times in the washing machine to get them really clean. Then they are spun very quickly to remove most of the water so that they may dry quickly. This forces droplets of water out of them by centrifugal force. After spin-drying, the clothes can be air-dried or dried in a tumble dryer.

Washing machines, now a days, are being used on a large scale. They save time and labour of washing the clothes.　　OOO

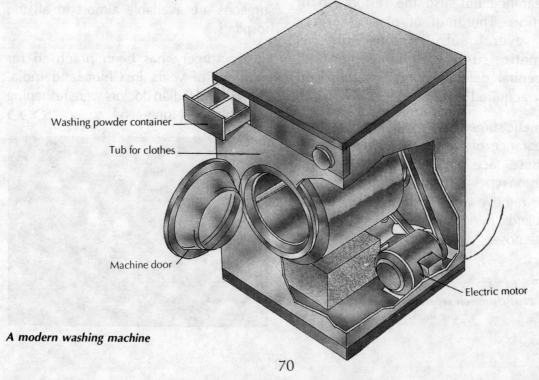

Washing powder container

Tub for clothes

Machine door

Electric motor

A modern washing machine

8

How does a dish washer work?

A dishwasher is a modern domestic appliance that cleans and dries utensils automatically. These machines generally worked on the principle of passing the dirty dishes under jets of hot water by means of conveyor belt or revolving basket. Modern dishwashers have reversed the procedure. In these dishwashers the utensils are cleaned by revolving jets of water above and below the basket.

A modern dishwasher contains heater, pumps, motors etc. and requires a water supply. It is housed in a enamelled cabinet. A drop down door enables the plastic coated basket to be pulled out on slides or rollers for loading. The door is fitted with a microswitch to shut of all operations. A modern dishwasher is shown in the figure.

A dish washer generally has several programmes which may be selected by means of keys or push buttons, depending on the type of utensils to be washed and the type of food residues to be removed. In a typical programme, dirty crockery and cutlery are loaded into specially designed carriers. To wash and rinse, water is sprayed from above and below the dish basket by whirling arms through which the water is pumped, each of the arms have several spray holes in it. The pressure of the water itself makes the jets spin around. The first part of the cycle uses water containing detergent to dissolve grease and grime. The detergent is loaded into a compartment in the lid which automatically releases the right amount at the proper point in the cycle. In the second part of the cycle, clean water rinses away the soapy water. Then a heating element warms and dries the utensils.

A timing device automatically controls the selected cycle, it is often operated by means of round calibrated knob. Some machines have pilot lights which indicate the part of the cycle in operation. These machines are proving very useful as kitchen aids.

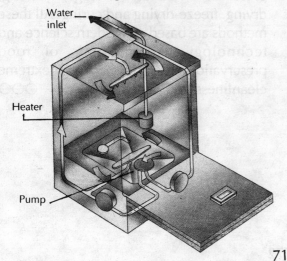

Water inlet

Heater

Pump

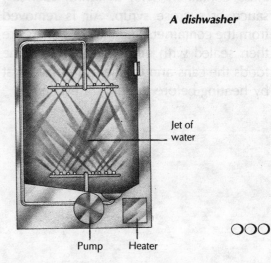

A dishwasher

Jet of water

Pump   Heater

OOO

9

How is food packed in cans?

Canning of food is one of the methods of food preservation. The food that is stored in cans has to be made sterile and free from germs to keep it fresh. Canning also involves keeping air away from food because it would bring germs to it.

In a canning factory, the food is prepared in large containers. It is heated to destroy micro-organisms and to stop enzyme activity. Most germs-killing temperatures range from 100°C to 121°C. Meat, fish and vegetables are heated at about 120°C. The sterilizing time depends on the temperature, the container and the type of food.

The food after heating goes to the canning machine, which is fed with a line of empty cans. The food is filled in the metal or glass containers with a liquid, such as, sauce or sucrose syrup. Air is removed from the containers and the containers are then sealed with air-tight lids. For some foods the cans and food are sterilized first by heating before the cans are filled.

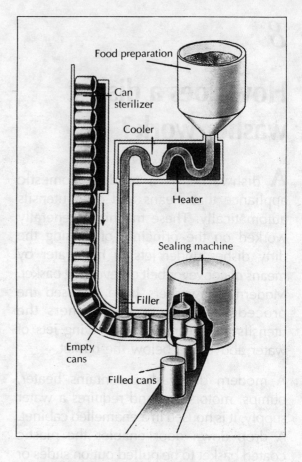

A machine filling and sealing the cans

Most canned food can be kept for more than a year. The other methods of food preservation are cold storage, freezing, drying, freeze-drying and curing. All these methods are based on modern science and technology. All methods of food preservation are performed with extreme cleanliness and hygienically.   OOO

10

What is star Television?

Star television is the popular name of satellite television. A broadcasting transmitter on the ground can transmit signals only to a limited distance. Even if the transmitting antenna is on a tall mast, hills and valleys in the landscape can soon block the signals. The television satellite can be taken as an antenna on an incredibly tall mast — so tall that it is in space.

Satellites are being used for many years by TV stations to exchange TV programmes among each other. The signals are beamed out from earth station to space which are picked up by the aerial of the satellite. These signals are re-transmitted by the satellite down to another part of the earth where they are received by the dish antenna. The receiving TV station then transmits the signals to viewers in the usual way. In this way, TV signals are sent from one part of the world to the other. TV transmission from one earth station to the satellite and back to another earth station is shown in the figure. Sports events are transmitted in this way.

The latest development is direct broadcasting by satellite, known as D.S.B., where the signals go straight to the viewers. For this, you need a special dish aerial like the one shown here to pick up D.S.B. TV.

OOO

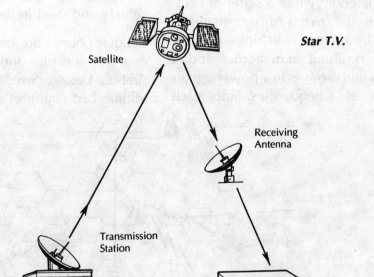

Satellite

Star T.V.

Receiving Antenna

Transmission Station

T.V.

11

What is a cellular phone ?

Cellular telephone or radio telephone is a type of mobile telephone which is integrated with existing telephone systems, allowing mobile users to contact any one with a standard telephone and vice-versa. Each mobile telephone has its own number which can be dialled from any other telephone. The cellular telephone can cover the entire country, even inter-continental telephone calls are possible with cellular telephone.

A cellular telephone network is setup by dividing the country into a series of cells, each with its own radio transmitter controlled by a central switching computer. Each cell is about 5km across and it broadcasts and receives low power signals on its own set of frequencies. Since each cell is so small, the same set of frequencies can be reused in any other cell whose transmitter's range does not overlap the first cell. As a cellular telephone is mobile and moves from one cell to another, the braodcast frequency needs to be changed.

Cellular radio phone signals follow a route starting from the mobile, then of the radio transmitter. The signal is sent along the coventional telephone lines to an exchange. The analog signal is converted to digital signal, ready for switching to the correct destination. After switching, the signal is reconverted to analog and sent along telephone lines to the destination transmitter, where it is transmitted and consequently received by another mobile.

There are at present three types of cellular telephones. These are — automobile based, pocket or briefcase portables and transportables which can be moved in a vehicle and used in the hand.

Cellular phones are being used by many countries besides India such as Saudi Arabia, U.S.A., Sweden, Britain, Japan, Middle East countries etc.   ○○○

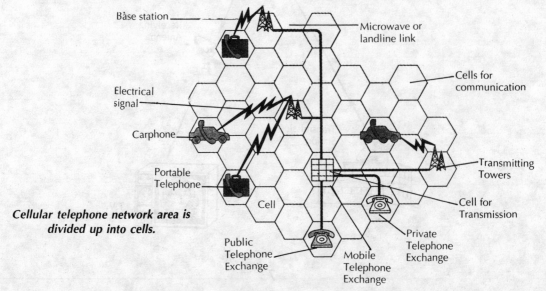

Cellular telephone network area is divided up into cells.

Base station — Microwave or landline link — Cells for communication — Electrical signal — Carphone — Portable Telephone — Cell — Transmitting Towers — Cell for Transmission — Public Telephone Exchange — Mobile Telephone Exchange — Private Telephone Exchange

12

How are skyscrapers built?

Skyscrapers are tall buildings that tower in the air. The foundations of a skyscraper are laid by drilling holes in the ground and filling them with concrete. If the ground is firm, the foundations are wide so that they will spread the weight of the building and they do not go very deep. If the ground is not very firm, deep shafts of concrete are driven into the ground to anchor the skyscraper firmly.

Then a frame of steel griders or concrete beams is erected, often with a pillar like concrete core containing lift shafts and stairs. The frame and core take all the weight of the building so that the walls do not have to support the floors above.

The tallest skyscraper of the world is the Sears Tower of Chicago state (Illinois) with 110 storeys rising 443 meter. The other famous skyscraper is National Westminster Tower of Great Britain. OOO

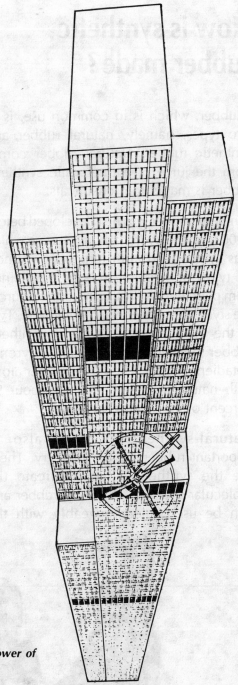

Tallest skyscraper of the world, The Sears Tower of Chicago state.

13

How is synthetic rubber made?

Rubber, which is in common use, is of two types, namely, natural rubber and synthetic rubber. Natural rubber comes from the juice of a tree while synthetic rubber is made from chemicals.

Synthetic rubber was first developed before 1900 from the hydrocarbon isoprene which was synthesized from turpentine. Almost all types of synthetic rubber is obtained from petroleum industry. Important sources are styrene, acetylene and butadiene. Two of the most important types of synthetic rubber are butyl rubber and styrene-butadiene rubber. These two rubber along with natural rubber, made up about 90 percent of the worlds' demand.

Natural-synthetic rubber is also an important rubber for the industry. These are the synthetics that duplicate the molecular structure of natural rubber and can be used interchangeably with the natural product. Since World War II, a lot of products such as foam rubber, have been directly made from natural rubber latex or from synthetic equipment.

Chemists have developed better and better synthetic rubber with different properties. Neoprene rubbers resist oxygen, sunlight, gasoline, oil and other chemicals better than natural rubber does. Nitrile rubber which stands heat upto 177°C is much better than natural rubber. It is used in gasoline hose, leather products and many types of cloth. Polysulphide rubbers such as thiokol have great resistance to softening and swelling in gasoline and greases. Polyurethane rubbers resist age and heat and withstand remarkable stresses and pressures. Silicone rubbers keep their like properties at much higher and lower temperatures than natural rubber. Silicone rubbers are used in seals, gaskets, and jet plane industry. These rubbers are made of oxygen and silicon with a hydro-carbon added to the silicone. Thermoplastic rubbers are used as shoe soles and automotive parts.

Rubber whether natural or synthetic, is one of the most versatile materials available to industry. ○○○

Articles made from synthetic rubber

14

What is an Alkaline Battery?

A battery is a device that produces electricity by chemical action. A battery contains one or more units called cells. Each cell can produce current.

There are three main types of dry cell batteries: carbon-zinc, alkaline and mercury. Here we are describing an alkaline battery.

An alkaline dry cell battery is more powerful than carbon-zinc battery. It lasts five to eight times longer than a carbon-zinc battery. It has carbon and zinc as electrodes. Instead of a carbon rod extending from the top, a nail like collector (1) is inserted from the bottom. The granules of zinc which form the anode (2) are made uniform in size and shape. The electrolyte — a solution of potassium hydroxide — is in direct contact with the anode, ensuring that the anode is exhausted by the end of the battery's life. The manganese dioxide cathode (3) is made by electrolysis. The additional oxygen, increases the reactivity of the cell. Alkaline dry cells are used mainly for portable radios. ○○○

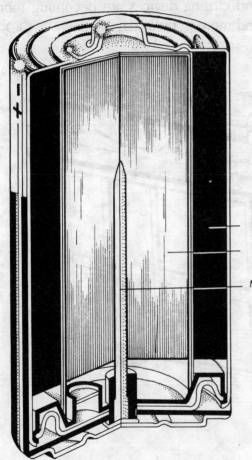

Anode collector

Granules of zinc

Mangnese dioxide cathode

Inside an alkaline battery

77

15

What is automatic door operation?

Scientists have developed the devices by which a door can be opened or closed automatically. There are three common ways of operating automatic doors: (1) by actuating a pressure pad on the surface in front of the door, (2) by cutting a light beam located in a wall near the door and (3) by actuating a wall mounted manual pressure pad like a switch (figure).

Automatic doors are powered by various drive systems — some are totally electric, some are electromechanical and others are pneumatic. Various door opening actions are available such as automatic slide with or without manual swing out side panels for use when the automatic doors are locked or turned off; single or double swing doors and side and swing combinations. Automatic door opening and closing devices are becoming more and more popular day by day.   OOO

1. Pressure pad
2. Light beam
3. Pressure pad in switch form

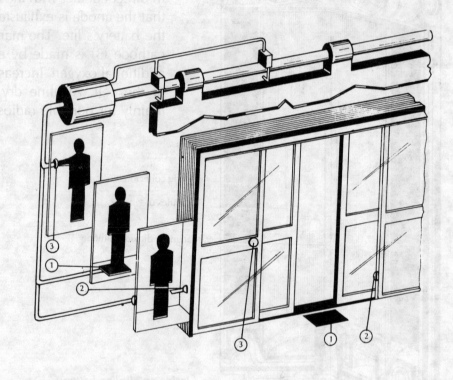

The operating of an automatic door

16

What is the remote control of a television set?

The remote control is a small hand-held device used by a viewer to control the television without touching its controls. It is an opto-electronic device which makes use of optical and electronic techniques and hardware.

The remote control device emits a beam of light which is detected by a, "light control" built into the television. In an optical remote controller, a multivator (1) produces pulses (2) from push button controls (3). The pulses are amplified (4) and modulate a beam of light in the form of saw tooth pulses (5) These pulses are received by a photo transistor (6) fitted in the television set, amplified (7) and used as a trigger to recreate the pulse shape (8) The resulting signals are used to change volume and channels.

The volume, contrast and channel can be altered by remote control. If the television is connected to a video cassette recorder, programmes can be recorded and replayed by remote control. A remote control prevents the wear and tear of switch buttons.   OOO

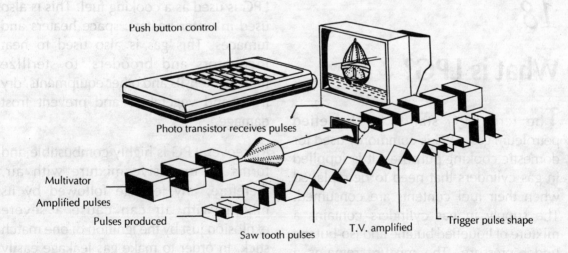

Push button control

Photo transistor receives pulses

Multivator

Amplified pulses

Pulses produced

Saw tooth pulses

T.V. amplified

Trigger pulse shape

An optional remote controller

17

How does a steam iron work?

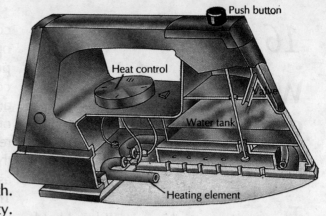

The inside of a steam iron

A hot iron smooths out creases in cloth. Most irons are powered by electricity. Inside the iron is an electric heater. A steam iron provides heat and steam at the same time for ironing many different fabrics. Steam makes the cloth slightly damp which helps to remove creases and wrinkles because moisture softens the fibres in the material and makes them flexible.

A steam iron contains a water tank in which water is boiled by the heating element to make steam. A push-button on top of the iron opens a valve to let the steam through the holes on the cloth being ironed. With the button up, no steam gets through to the cloth and the iron works like an ordinary iron. OOO

18

What is LPG?

The term LPG stands for liquefied petroleum gas. LPG is commonly used for domestic cooking purposes. It is supplied in gas cylinders that need to be replaced when their fuel contents are consumed. The supply in gas cylinders contains a mixture of liquefied butane and iso-butane under pressure. The mixture remains a liquid under pressure but the highly volatile liquid fuel in the cylinder evaporates when pressure is released. The gaseous mixture starts going into the burner of attached stove or oven. Here it is ignited and the blue flame is used for different purposes.

LPG is used as a cooking fuel. This is also used in water heaters, space heaters and furnaces. This gas is also used to heat incubators and brooders, to sterilize milking utensils and other equipments, dry fruits and vegetables and prevent frost damage.

Moreover, LPG is highly combustible and forms an explosive mixture with air, therefore, any leakage followed by its mixing with air can cause a severe explosion just by the ignition of one match stick. In order to make gas leakage easily detectable some strong smelling substance is added to LPG. Before igniting the match stick we should be sure that there is no such smell near the gas cylinder or in the kitchen. OOO

19

What is bar code?

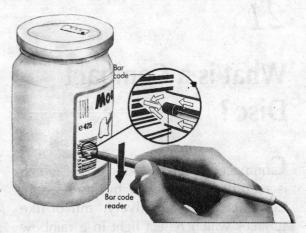

The functioning of a bar code

A bar code is computerized information encoded in a pattern of black and white stripes. The black and white lines represent IS and OS and can be read by light. They carry encoded information — from the membership number of a sports club to the price and stock number of a packet of washing powder in a supermarket. In fact bar codes are used to store data of all kinds.

The code is scanned by a beam of light. When a beam of light is passed over the bar code only the white stripes reflect back the light. This is picked up by a photo-detector which produces a pulse of electricity when it receives light. So the black and white bar code is translated into on/off pulses of electricity. These pulses are fed into a computer for decoding. Now a days laser beams are being used for reading the bar codes.   OOO

20

What is the principle of an autopilot?

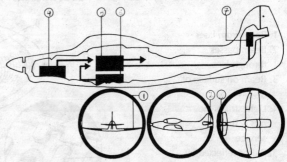

1. Ailerons control 'roll' 2. Elevators control 'pitch'
3. Rudder controls 'yaw' 4. Guroscopic altitude sensors
5. Computer 6. Radio or radar receiver 7. Servo motor rudder

The principle of an Autopilot

ost large planes have an autopilot. This is a device operated by a computer. It will fly the place without the pilot's touching the controls. These autopilots can even control take offs and landings.

The principle of an automatic pilot is similar to the automatic steering of ships, but here three gyroscopic sensors and their associated equipment are used to control the three variables in aircraft position. These three variables are yaw, pitch and roll. The complex autopilot system uses an airborne computer which activates servomotors for introducing necessary corrections. A radio or radar link to the computer allows control from the ground for automatic takeoffs and landings.

OOO

21

What is a Compact Disc?

Compact disc is a new kind of disc which is recorded and played by laser beam. Compact disc has silvery, mirror-like surfaces which reflect light in a rainbow spectrum. The music disc is about 12 cm dia. while video disc is about the size of an LP and hold both pictures and sound.

In the recording process, sound signals are converted into number so that each part of the signal has a precise code. These numbers are recorded as the binary digits 0 and 1. Physically, sound is recorded on a CD as a series of minute pits and flats which relate to the two digits.

The laser disc has a very reflective metallic surface, covered by a protective coating of clear plastic. A semiconductor or small He-Ne laser is used for scanning. The player spins the disc and scans with laser beam which moves straight across the disc from the centre to the edge. The shiny surface reflects the beam back into the player, where it is picked up by electronic device. This produces an electrical signal which the player decodes back into video pictures and sounds. The laser beam reads about 20,000 digits every second which are converted into sound signals.

The biggest advantage of compact discs is that they never wear out because there is no physical contact between the disc and the player — only a beam of light. ○○○

1. Beam from laser
2. Beam passes through lens
3. Beam on surface of disc
4. Light strikes the pits & flats on service
5. Pulses reflected by prism
6. Pulses focus on light sensitive cell

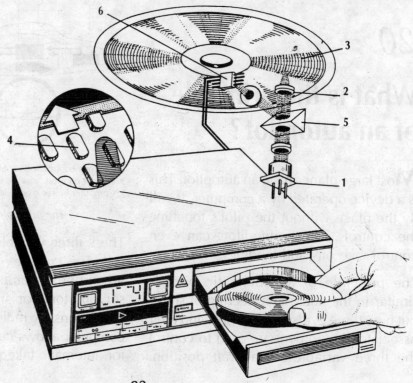

A compact disc-player

3
Plants & Animals

• How can an Owl see clearly at night? • Do Ants also have their kingdoms ? • Why does the dog go mad? • Why do the eyes of some animals shine in the dark? • How far can a Kangaroo jump? • What is a Virus? • What is Fungus? • What are bacteria? • What is regeneration? • Is Bamboo a tree or grass? • How do some creatures make a shell on their body? • How do animals and plants survive in deserts? • How do migratory birds find their way? • Can animals reason? • How do plants take and make their food? • How is bark formed?• Why can't animals talk like us?

1

How can an Owl see clearly at night?

An owl is a bird of prey with large head and eyes, short neck, broad wings and sharp claws. About 130 species of owls are found around the world. In some countries, they are treated as in auspicious birds, while in others, they are regarded as symbol of wealth and wisdom. What is peculiar about owl is that they can see more clearly at night than during the day. In fact they "come to life" at night and are an apt example of 'nocturnal' birds. Birds which can see more clearly at night rather than during the day, are known as nocturnal birds. On the other hand, birds which have a clearer vision along the day time than during night are called 'diurnal'.

You must be very curious as to how nocturnal birds in general and owls in particular can see so clearly at night.

To understand this, it is essential to know how we see things. Light scattered by an object is focused on to the screen of the eyes by the lenses inside the eyes. This screen of the eyes is called the retina. An inverted image of the object is formed on the retina which is carried to the brain by optic nerves. This is erected by the brain and thus we see the object.

The owl's eyes have four special features due to which it can see more clearly at night. Firstly, the distance between the lens of its eye and the retina is more than the distance in the case of human eyes. Due to this, the image formed on the retina is bigger in size. Secondly, the number of 'rods' and 'cones' (special cells which help in the vision) in the retina is very large— almost 10,000 per sq mm compared to 2,000 per sq mm in our eyes. Thus, the owl can see five times more than us. Thirdly, its eyes have a red coloured material, chemically a protein, which makes its eyes more sensitive to light. Fourthly, the pupils of its eyes can dilate more, thus allowing even the smallest amount of light to enter into the eyes. Because of these four factors, the owl can see more clearly in darkness. Due to the extreme sensitivity of their eyes to light, objects appear too bright and uncomfortable to the eyes in the bright light of the day. Surprisingly enough, an owl can rotate its head by 180° i.e. it can see at the back of his head. ○○○

2

Do Ants also have their kingdoms ?

A colony of ants and the queen ant

Eggs   Larvae   Ant

Ants are insects that belong to the order Hymenoptera. More than two thousand species of ants have been studied by scientists. Ants are found in most parts of the world. Most ants are smaller than an inch.

Ants are social animals and have their own kingdoms. This means that they live together in large colonies or groups. Some colonies may contain millions of ants. Most colonies make nests in the ground or in dead trees.

There are three kinds of ants in each colony — queens, laying eggs; males who do not work; and a corps of female workers. An ant colony contains too many cells or chambers for different purposes. The queen lives in one, laying eggs. Next door is the hatching room, from which the grubs as they turn into pupae are carried into another room to develop. The other rooms are used for special purposes such as storing food etc. An ant colony may contain several queens each with its own suite of rooms. Worker ants collect food, feed the young ants and build the nest. Some species of ants also have female soldier ants. They protect the nest.

The army of ants of the tropical jungles march to a different place everyday. Thousands of them march in a narrow band and eat any animal that comes in their way. Army ants can eat all the flesh off the bones of a dead animal very quickly.

Ants can do many things. They are able to travel long distances away from their nest and find their way back, because they follow their own chemical trails. Ants are very strong. They can lift things that weigh 50 times more than their own. OOO

Ants

85

3

Why does the dog go mad ?

Dog is regarded as a faithful animal. But when it goes mad it becomes very dangerous. If a mad dog bites someone, it leads to his death if not treated properly.

A dog goes mad when it suffers from a disease called 'rabies'. This disease is caused by a virus which is carried by air or by some wild animals and enters the dog's body through a wound in its skin. The virus is bullet shaped having a diameter of about 70 millimicrons and a length of about 210 millimicrons. It moves from the saliva to the infected wounds and through sensory nerves to the central nervous system, multiplies there and then destroy brain cells. The dog becomes lazy, suffers from fever and loses all interest in food. In about 4-6 weeks, when these viruses affect the dog's brain, the dog gets excited. It growls and barks and saliva froths from the mouth. During this period, the dog can bite anybody. This is the stage when the dog is said to be mad. After these symptoms appear, it is likely to die within 3 to 5 days. Some infected dogs do not go mad but show signs of paralysis, called 'dumb rabies.'

When a mad dog bites a man, the virus present in its saliva enters man's body through the wound. Initially the victim experiences mental weakness and uneasiness which is followed by fever. He suffers from lack of sleep and feels frightened. The muscles in his throat get slackened and he faces difficulties in swallowing food or liquid. He is afraid of water. That is why this condition is also called 'hydrophobia' which means 'fear of water'. These signs appear in the victim within one to three months after dog's bite. In cases of dog-bite, the affected portions should be immediately cleaned and anti-rabies injections should be given to the victim within three days of the bite, the number of injections varying from 3 to 14 depending on the location and number of bites.

The virus of rabies also attacks foxes, jackals, monkeys, cats and rats because they have the least contact with us.

4

Why do the eyes of some animals shine in the dark?

Have you ever seen a cat sitting in the dark? Though its body is not visible, yet its yellow eyes shine in the darkness. The eyes of tiger, leopard, lion etc. also shine in the darkness or night just like the eyes of a cat. Besides these, there are many other animals whose eyes shine in the dark.

Eyes of cats, tigers, lions, leopards etc. shine in the night

The eyes of these animals have a thin layer of a special crystalline substance which reflects the light falling on it. This reflected light is the cause of the shine. In the night, even the smallest amount of light falling on this crystalline surface gets reflected and thus we see the shining eyes. Animals with such eyes who can see things clearly in darkness are called nocturnal animals.

Studies made on cats have shown that behind the retina of eyes, there is a crystalline layer called the 'luminous tapetum', which reflects light. Due to this layer the cat can see clearly in dim light and its eyes shine in the dark when the light is directed on them. Many animals do not have this crystalline layer, hence their eyes do not shine in the dark.

It has been observed that the colour of the shine is different in different animals. It depends upon the number of blood vessels present in their eyes. If the number of blood vessels is large, the colour of the shine is red and if the number of blood vessels is small the colour of the shine is white or pale yellow. OOO

5

How far can a Kangaroo jump?

Kangaroos are marsupials (animals with pouches) that live in Australia and New Guinea. Most of them live on grassy plains and feed on plants. They move about in troops, springing along on their big, powerful hind legs and large feet. Their long tails help them to balance.

There are five species of kangaroos. Red and grey ones are the largest. A red kangaroo may be taller and heavier than a man. Grey kangaroos can bounce along at 40 kilometres per hour if chased. Wallaroos are smaller kind of kangaroo.

A full grown kangaroo stands about six feet tall. Its front legs are short while the hind legs are very long. The powerful hind legs enable the kangaroo to take long jumps of 3 to 5 metres at a time. if a hunter or hunting dog chases a kangaroo, it runs very fast making long jumps. It can cover a distance of 7 to 9 metres just in one jump. When a kangaroo is cornered by hunting dogs, it can seize a dog with its forelegs and kill it with one swing of its hind legs.

The female kangaroo has a pouch in its belly in between the hind legs in which it keeps its young ones till they grow up. When a baby kangaroo is born, it is a tiny, pink, naked mass of about 2.5 cm in length

The red kangaroo is the largest of all marsupials

and about 1 gm in weight. Not only the infant kangaroo, but even young kangaroos need the protection of their mothers. A kangaroo lives on the mother's milk until it leaves the pouch at the age of 6 to 8 months. A kangaroo lives for about 6 to 8 years. Finding the young ones in danger, the mother kangaroo lifts them with its mouth and places them inside its pouch.

The kangaroo is a mild animal like the sheep and goats. Like the hare, it is unable to see an object just in front of it. But its power of smelling and hearing is quite strong. ooo

6

What is a Virus ?

Viruses are micro organisms which cause various diseases in all types of living bodies, so much so that even bacteria are affected by viruses. There is a helpful virus called bacteriophage which eats bacteria and can not be seen by necked eye. One can only see them with the help of an electron or ultra microscope. Strangely enough, viruses are considered both as living and non-living objects. They grow and multiply in living cells and therefore are treated as living organisms. Since they do not grow outside living cells. they are classified as non-living objects also. Consequently, they are treated on the border line of living and non-living matter.

Viruses were first discovered by Mayer in 1888. He found them on tobacco leaves. There are many kinds of viruses. They are of varying shapes and sizes. Some are long as rods, some are hexagonal. The smallest viruses are of the size of a millionth part of an inch. They are found in the cells of plants, animals and human beings. They are born in these cells, multiply there and spread diseases.

Viruses spread many diseases amongst human beings, animals, plants and trees. Different viruses spread different diseases. Small-pox, chicken-pox, polio, mumps, influenza, hepatitis, measles, jaundice, trochoma in eyes, etc. are among the main diseases spread by them. Some of them cause brain diseases such as paralysis and rabies. Some kinds of cancer too are caused by viruses. Many diseases in the plants of tomatoes, bananas, sugar-cane, lemon and cotton are also caused by them. Thus we see that they are among the greatest enemies of living beings.

Most of the viruses die at high or low temperature. However, some of them are immune to the variations in temperature. Chlorine and hydrochloric acid are used to kill them. There is very little doctors can do to treat viral diseases directly. Our body fights viruses in two ways — by producing antibodies and interferon. Antibodies clump viruses and destroy them. Interferon helps keep viruses from spreading cell to cell. Many vaccines have been developed to give artificial immunity against viral diseases. OOO

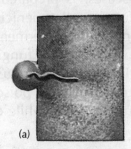
(a)

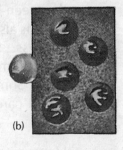
(b)

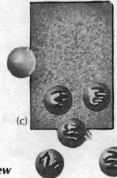
(c)

(a) Virus entering a cell
(b) New viruses being made
(c) Cell bursts open and new viruses are released

89

7

What is Fungus?

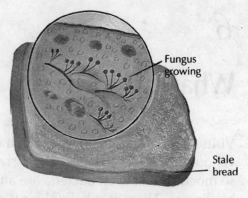

Fungus growing

Stale bread

Growth of fungi on a stale bread

In rainy season, you must have seen the growth of soft, white, cottony and velvety patches of mould on stale bread, pickles, damp cloth, leather, food, leaves, fruits and vegetables. These are called fungi and are classified flowerless plants having no roots, no stems and no leaves and are without chlorophyll—the green colouring matter. Due to the lack of chlorophyll, fungi depend for their food either on a living organizm (parasite) or on the dead organic matter (saprophyte). When we examine the fungi under a microscope, we see that they consist of a large number of black, green, yellow or blue fibres. These fibres have two parts—one part is mycellium which spreads like roots and takes food from the material on which it grows. The other part is round, ball-like lymph, which contains spores. Always present in the air, they start multiplying whenever they get bread, fruits and other eatables in hot and humid places.

Fungi feed on dead plants or vegetable matter. There are various kind of fungi: mushroom, mucor, mucedo (on bread), yeast, penicillium, mildus, rusts, blight etc.

They are both useful as well as harmful for us. The biggest advantage of fungi is that they destroy and eliminate useless organic matter by setting decay in them. The matter decomposes into oxygen, nitrogen, carbon, phosphorus etc. and they spread in the atmosphere. They also help in preparing bread, beer, wine and cheese; in making organic acids, enzymes, vitamins and antibiotics. Penicillin which is useful in curing many diseases, is prepared from the green-blue fungus called penicillium. Yeast is also a fungus, used in fermentation process. Some varieties of fungi like mushroom, gorrils, trafills etc. are used as food. Some mushrooms are poisonous hence care should be taken while eating them.

However, on the other hand, some of the fungi cause diseases in plants and trees and destroy crops of potato, apple, etc.

Poisonous Mushroom

8

What are bacteria?

Bacteria belong to the lowest category of plants. They are unicellular micro-organisms. They are as small as 25,000th part of an inch. Some of them are even smaller and cannot be seen with the help of an ordinary microscope. They reproduce through the process of cell division (fission) i.e. one cell divides itself into two. Under favourable circumstances the rate of their reproduction increases. Within twenty minutes the cells of the new bacterium divide into two, In forty minutes one bacterium multiplies to four and to sixty four in two hours. In this way, in twenty-four hours, one bacterium multiplies into 4,000,000,000,000 bacteria. If the rate of the reproduction of bacteria remains the same, the weight of the bacteria produced within 72 hours will become 33,000 times more than the weight of the earth. But this is impossible because in the struggle for food and water only one percent of them can survive. They may live in soil, water, air or in any other organisms.

Bacteria can be broadly classified into four types. Some bacteria are round, they are called coccus. The rod-shaped are called bacillus, spiral-shaped the spirillum and the comma-shaped vibrio.

Bacteria are both harmful and useful. They spread many diseases in human beings, animals and plants. Typhoid, tetanus, T.B., cholera, diphtheria, dysentry, whooping cough etc. are some of the well-known diseases which are spread by bacteria. But, on the other hand, some bacteria are very useful for mankind. Conversion of milk into curd is done by bacteria. They destroy the dead plants and animals by setting decay in them. Vinegar is also prepared by them. It is the bacteria which make yeast for bread, and colours the hides (animal skin). Certain antibiotics are also prepared by using them. Thus, bacteria are both useful and harmful to us. Antibiotics and sulpha drugs are used to control bacterial diseases.   ∘∘∘

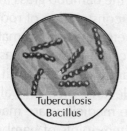

Tuberculosis Bacillus

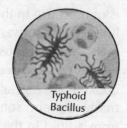

Typhoid Bacillus

Spirillum Undula

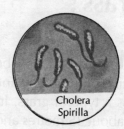

Cholera Spirilla

Four types of bacteria

9

What is regeneration ?

Would it not be wonderful if people who lost an arm or a leg or even a finger in an accident could simply grow another one in its place? But in reality it does not happen so in case of human beings. However, you will be surprised to know that there are some living beings in which a new limb develops at the same point from where the original limb has been lost. Development of a new body part in place of a lost one is known as regeneration.

If a small arm of a starfish is cut off or destroyed, it is regenerated. The hydra, lizards, sponges, newts and earthworm also possess this capability of regeneration.

The ability of regeneration is different in different creatures. Living beings with complicated structures have lesser ability of regeneration. Man and other mammals have a complex constitution. That is why they have lesser ability of regeneration. Mammals can replace hair, nails and skin. Mammals can also repair broken bones and other damaged tissues. Regrowing of the wings of birds is another example of regeneration.

In some species new tissues grow from the surface of the wound replacing the lost or damaged tissues. Sometimes, the tissues that an organism regenerate are different from the original ones. The regenerated structure may be smaller and weaker than the original one. ◯◯◯

10

Is Bamboo a tree or grass ?

Majority of people believe bamboo to be a kind of shrub or plant. In fact, it is neither. It is a type of grass. It can reach a height of about 35 metres and upto a thickness of about 30 cm. It has many varieties. About 600 species of bamboo have been studied. All kinds of bamboos have smooth, hard and strong trunks. The rate of their growth is very fast. It can grow up at the rate of 40 cm a day. One bamboo reportedly grew 90 cm in 24 hours. Some bamboos blossom only once in 30 years. Others may take 100 years to blossom. A bamboo plant dies after it blooms. The seeds from these blossoms grow into new plants.

It is only the stem of the bamboo grass that is of most use in the construction of roofs, huts, walls, houses, etc. It is used to make mats, baskets, musical pipes, paper, as a fishing rod and weapon for defence; it is cooked as vegetable and pickle is also made of them; some medicines are made from a fluid in the stem joints of bamboo branches. Its hollowed stems are used as water pipes especially in Japan.

It is found in abundance in South-East Asia, Indian subcontinent and the islands of the Pacific Ocean. ◯◯◯

11

How do some creatures make a shell on their body?

Oyester

Snail

Some fresh-water shells

You must have heard the sound of conch (shankh) blowing in the temples. You must have also seen big and small conches at sea-shores and on the river banks. Some conches are so small that they can be seen only with the help of a magnifying lens, whereas there are others as big as measuring up to 120 cm.

Do you know what these conches are and how they are formed? They are the body shells of aquatic creatures. These creatures are called mollusks. Some 60,000 species of the mollusks have so far been studied by the scientists. As the size of the mollusk increases, the outer shell also increases and becomes harder. They are made up of calcium carbonate (lime). The mollusk collects lime from the sea water and deposits it in its outer shell. When the mollusk dies, the shell floats and comes to the surface of water.

The shell of the mollusk has three main layers. The outer layer of the shell is made up of smooth material like the oyster and contains absolutely no lime. The layer below this i.e. the second layer is made up of calcium carbonate. The lowest layer that is the third layer, is a group of many thin layers, which are made up of oyster-like material and calcium carbonate. The conches are of many colours. They have many stains and stripes. These stains, colours and stripes have their origin in some colourful materials present in the glands of the mollusk. These colours, stripes and stains enhance the beauty of the conches.

The conches not only protect the mollusk, but they are also very useful for us. In ancient times people used mollusk shells as coins. Small conches are even used as part of necklaces. They are used as decoration pieces in homes. Buttons are made from small shells. Aquatic animals with shells have been existing for billions of years. After their death these shells deposit themselves on the sea-bed which form rocks of limestone. ◯◯◯

12

How do animals and plants survive in deserts?

Due to the scarcity of water and particular climatic conditions (hot, dry, windy) prevailing in the desert, it is very difficult for animals as well as plants to survive. Nonetheless, we do find some of these. These are adapted to the desert conditions. Let us see what types of vegetation and animals are found there and how do they survive.

The vegetation of a desert is mainly thorny shrubs, cacti and palm (especially date) trees. Cacti and other desert plants have adapted themselves to live in desert conditions. They have evolved ways to store water in their fleshy stems. The leaves have squeazed themselves into tiny thorns to reduce the loss of water. The roots go deep into the ground and are wide spread to collect every drop of water available. The stem stores the water and slowly gets thinner as the water gets used up. In some cacti the thorns are pointed towards the earth. The dew drops deposited on the ends fall on the earth hence moisture is maintained below the cacti. There are quite a few animals found in deserts such as snails, pack rat, jerboa, etc. Most desert animals sleep during the day to escape the

The animal and plant life present in the desert

day temperature and they come out in night in search of food. Some animals sleep during the hottest part of the year. Animals such as kangaroo, rat and gerbil can survive with little or no water. Reptiles adjust their body temperatures to cope with heat and cold. The Australian desert toad stores water in its body. Some lizards, ants, owls and snakes also live in deserts. OOO

13

How do migratory birds find their way?

Every spring millions of birds migrate from their winter quarters to the temperate regions of the world to breed. These regions abound with food on which the parents can rear their hungry chicks.

The biggest migrations are to the northerly parts of North America, Europe and Asia. But there is some migration to the southern hemisphere too. For example the double-banded dotterel flies from Australia to New-Zealand to breed. The American golden Plover undertakes a non stop flight of 3325 km between Alaska and Hawaii. In the northern hemisphere wild geese fly north to their breeding grounds in the spring and fly south in the autumn.

Migration is mainly triggered off by changes in the length of the day, which cause a change in the bird's hormone balance.

Now the question is how do the birds find their way while migrating from a place and then returning to their original place?

Some birds may learn from their parents. They make the first migration with the older birds which have made the trip before. These younger birds teach their young the migration route the next year. Some birds may guide themselves by landmarks, such as mountains, lakes and

Swallows must cross the Sahara Desert

they must find food as they fly

Many birds migrate when the season changes. Figure shows the migration of swallows

coast-lines. Others may use the sun and stars to navigate by, because when the sky is cloudy, they often get hopelessly lost. Scientists still do not know how all migratory birds find their way.

Birds are not the only animals that migrate. Many fish, mammals, flying insects, locusts, eels also migrate. ○○○

95

14

Can animals reason?

It is generally believed that animals don't have reasoning power, but it is not true. They do have power of reasoning but compared to human beings, it is very small. Amongst the animals themselves, the degree of reasoning varies.

Some experiments have led to the conclusion that monkeys and apes have better reasoning than other animals. An experiment was conducted to test the reasoning power of the monkeys. In this experiment two wooden boxes were placed in a room and a bunch of bananas was hanged at a height beyond the reach of the monkeyes. When a monkey was left in the room, it looked at the bunch for some time and then looked at the boxes. It put one box over another and then climbed on them. Thus, it was able to pluck the bunch of bananas. This proved that the monkeys could think how to use the boxes to get the bananas. Again, a monkey is an animal who can also discriminate among colours. It can be trained and taught to learn many things.

Scientists believed that dogs, cats and some other animals can also use their reason upto some extent. For instance, the pet dogs, if taught, can learn many things. You might have seen a bear show in which the bear acts according to the commands of his master. It is obvious that it uses its memory in its performance. Birds are always on the lookout for food. Whenever they see any food stuff, they fly down and lift it. The lizard again approaches its prey very cautiously and carefully. This proves that the lizard uses its reason to capture its prey.

If you look at the birds' nests, you have to concede that certain amount of reasoning has definitely gone into their formation. These nests have special arrangements for regulating heat and light. They are fabricated for laying eggs and protecting the young ones. ooo

Chimpanzee trying to open a safe containing food, shows its intelligence

15

How do plants take and make their food?

It is a well-known fact that trees and plants are also living beings like humans. They need food, water and air for survival. It is interesting to know how they take their food.

Plants derive their food both from the earth and the air. If you minutely look at their roots, you will find that the ends of these roots are like fine fibres. We call them root-hairs. They absorb water and minerals and transport them upwards to the leaves through the trunk and the branches. It is the leaves which prepare the food.

The leaves have pores which are filled with air. They also have a green colouring matter called chlorophyll. This chlorophyll acts as a catalyst, and uses carbon of the carbon dioxide and the hydrogen of the water present in the leaves to make carbohydrates (sugars). In this process oxygen and water are given out which are excreted by the leaves of plants.

Sugar is further converted into starch. From these carbohydrates, the plant can build up complex substances as foods which it needs for its life and growth. These substances include proteins, juices, oils (fats) etc. The water from which the plants take hydrogen for photosynthesis contains dissolved minerals needed in building

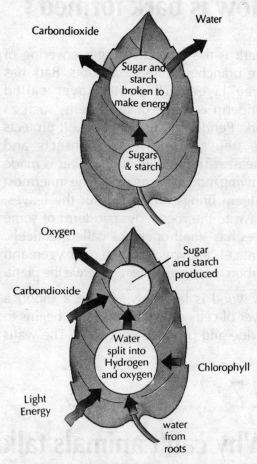

Process of photosynthesis taking place in the leaves of plants

various parts of the plant body. These are chiefly the compounds of nitrogen, sulphur, phosphorous, sodium, calcium, magnesium, iron etc.

Food not immediately needed for growth is stored in the plant including its seeds, fruits, tubers or bulbs. This accumulated food in the seed is used in its germination. ○○○

97

16

How is bark formed?

Bark is the protective outer covering of tree branches, trunks and roots. Bark has three layers. The outer layer called periderm is made of dead cells, such as cork. Periderm is usually thick. It protects the tree against weather, insects and diseases. The middle cortex layer is made of living, non growing cells. The innermost phloem brings food made in the leaves, down to the roots. The periderm of some trees has small openings called lenticels. Lenticels allow gases such as oxygen and carbon dioxide to enter and leave the plant.

As wood is laid down inside a shoot, a layer of cells near the outer side begins to divide and produce cork cells. The walls of these cells soon get heavily thickened with a waterproof substance. The cells die and form bark.

Over the years the bark is constantly added to form the inside of the tree. So as the diameter of the twig, branch or trunk increases, the waterproof barrier is maintained. But the outer bark often splits and cracks or becomes flaky.

As already mentioned, the bark protects a tree from the weather and sudden temperature changes. it contains substances that repel insects and resist fire. Bark often has commercial uses. The actual cork comes from the bark of the mediterranean cork oak. The drug Quinine is obtained from the bark of Cinchona trees and Cinnamon comes from the bark of the Cinnamon tree. Cough medicines and many other useful substances are also obtained from the bark. ○○○

17

Why can't animals talk like us?

In many stories it is told that animals can talk like us. But this is our imagination only. Amongst all the living beings, man is the only creature on earth who can communicate with the help of words or speech. This is because of the higher development of our brain. Because of a less developed brain, animals have not been able to originate words or a language to express their feelings. Hence they can't talk like we do.

It is a well-established fact that the animals too feel happiness, sorrow, fear, love, affection, hostility, hunger, thirst or protective needs etc. as humans do. Because they are incapable of expressing their feelings in words, they express or communicate to each other or to humans, with the help of certain gestures and sounds, which may or may not be familiar or understood by us. You might have seen when a cat goes near a group of birds, all the birds start chirping very loudly in a peculiar way. They actually express their fear that they may be caught by the cat. Similarly a dog expresses its anger by barking and its feelings of flattery by wagging its tail. A monkey demonstrates its anger by making peculiar sounds. ○○○

4
Human Body

How does our tongue tell us the taste? • Why don't women have beard? • How do we lose our memory? • How long can man survive without food? • What happens to our body in sleep? • What causes people to faint? • Why are people dwarf? • How do we remember things? • Why does man grow old? • What causes baldness in people? • Why are vitamins essential for us? • Why do we get fever? • How do bones mend? • How does a wound heal? • Which of the body parts can be replaced with artificial parts?

1

How does our tongue tell us the taste?

Man has five senses of perception—skin, ears, eyes, nose and tongue. The tongue tells us the taste of food and drink warns us if food has gone stale or is bad.

The tongue is located inside the mouth and is an important muscle in our body. It is red in colour. If you examine it minutely, you will see granular bumps or projections on its upper surface, sides and back. These are called papillae. These papillae contain groups of contact called taste buds (chemoreceptors) . They are composed of cells. Hair like fibres emerge at the upper side of our tongue. At the lower end of the tongue, they end in nerve fibres of cells. These join the nerves of taste that lead to the brain.

The 4 main tastes are — sweet, salty, sour and bitter. All other tastes are a combination of two or more of these. These 4 main tastes are felt by different portions of our tongue. For example, salty and sweet tastes are felt by the tip of our tongue. Similarly, sour taste is detected by the buds on the sides of the tongue and bitter taste, by the back portion of the tongue. The tongue is also sensitive to irritants such as pepper.

The taste of food is known only when it is in the liquid state. As we chew our food, a portion of it dissolves in the saliva. This dissolved form of the food activates the particular taste buds. These generate nerve impulses and the nerve fibres carry these messages to the "taste centre" in the brain. The brain then perceives the taste.

In addition to the tongue, our nose, which smells the food, also helps in perceiving the total taste of food. Smell is also a part of the taste. In the case of wine, cocoa and fruit juices, it is the smell which helps in the realization of the real taste. When liquids are taken into the mouth, the tongue

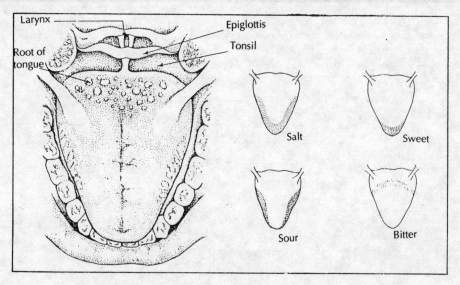

experiences the taste while their smell enters the nose and, through the "smell nerves", it reaches the brain. In this way is derived the total pleasure of taste.

When we suffer from cold, fever, or even constipation/indigestion, the taste buds get covered by some impurities and do not get properly activated. Heat of the body (in fever) or even hotness of food, also deactivates the taste buds. Hence, we do not perceive the real taste under such unhealthy conditions.

The number of taste buds on the tongue of an adult is about 3000 which is much more than that of a child. As we grow older, the taste buds start losing vitality and, finally, become inactive, thus decreasing in number. In a 70-year-old man, for example, the number of taste buds is only 40. The taste buds, like all skin cells, are constantly being replaced. About half of the taste buds are replaced every ten days.

OOO

2

Why don't women have beard ?

All mammals have some hair on their bodies and man is also a mammal. In some mammals hair cover the whole body but in humans, hair grow only in certain parts.

Hair on our body preserve the body warmth and protect the skin and body openings. They also help us in realising the sensation of physical touch. The hair on our eyebrows and eye lashes, ear and nose help guard these body cavities against dust and insects.

Now the question is, why do men have beards, and women do not? This can be understood as follows. When a child is born, he has only fur like hair on the body.

As he grows, hair become harder. Boys and girls reach puberty at the age of 11 to 13 years. There is faster growth of sex glands at this age. In man, the testes and other sex glands, produce a group of hormones known as 'androgens'. In woman, the ovaries and other sex glands, produce another group known as 'estrogens'. The function of the androgens is to regulate secondary male sex features such as the growth of facial and chest hair and deepening of the male voice at puberty. The function of the estrogens is to regulate secondary female features, such as the change in the size of breasts, growth of pubic hair and onset of the menstrual cycle. There are various other changes in men and women brought about by these hormones. For example female body becomes soft and tender whereas, male body turns hard and strong. A special group of hormones called the 'progestrogens'; are responsible for the regulation of pregnancy. Hence women do not have beards due to the absence of androgens.

OOO

3

How do we lose our memory?

Some people lose their memory after an accident or on hearing tragic news. Such people forget their past and even fail to recognise their close friends and relatives. So much so they even forget their own names. In psychology this condition is called 'amnesia'.

Amnesia is caused by many factors, such as, ead injury, mental shock, extreme tiredness, ill-effects of medicines, surgery of brain, psychological processes, old age and after effects of drinking. Whatever may be the reasons causing amnesia, its effect on the brain is almost the same in each case. Memory is said to be stored in the brain as a "memory trace". What makes up this trace is not known. According to one theory each experience sets up an oscillating pattern or wave of electrical excitation in a group of cells. Each learning experience generates its own pattern of excitation. A given neuron may participate in thousands of separate memories but its removal will not appreciably diminish any of them.

Memory is considered a three-part-system. Sensory information store (SIS), short-term memory (STM) and long term memory (LTM). The SIS forms an instant, but very temporary, storage of every piece of information that comes in. Information can last for only about three tenths of a second in the SIS. If it has not been selected and transferred to short-term memory within this time, it fades away.

Short-term memory is used for carrying information a person needs for a few seconds, but can afford to forget later. Two characteristics of short term memory prevent its use as a permanent information store. First concentration is required to maintain a particular piece of information in it. Second, it is able to store only six or seven items such as a seven digit telephone number.

For any information to be permanently stored, it has to be passed from short-term to long-term memory by the mechanism of rehearsal. The long-term memory has virtually unlimited capacity. It allows a person to remember events that have happened years before. Permanent memory takes place through structural changes in nerve cells caused by patterns of electrical activity in these cells.

When somebody suffers from amnesia, he forgets events either preceding it or following it. It can last for weeks, months or even for years. There are people who have lost memory for life. When memory is restored, one remembers all the forgotten things but forgets every event which took place during the period when one had lost memory. One thing is however certain that in spite of the restoration of memory, some after effects do remain, thereby weakening the memory. ○○○

4

How long can man survive without food?

Like air and water, food is also essential for all living beings. From the smallest insects to the biggest animals—all need food for their survival. So much so that even plants and trees can not live for long without food. Each person requires a certain amount of food daily, according to size, weight, age and amount of activity. Most of us feel upset if we skip just one meal, and if we try to go without food for 12 hours we would really be uncomfortable.

Energy required for doing work is obtained from food. Cells and tissues damaged in doing work are repaired and replaced by it. It is very much needed for the growth and development of the body. In short, food is very essential for the proper functioning of the body.

Now the question arises: how long can we survive without food? There are some animals which can store food in their bodies and live on it for a long time. It has been observed that the smaller and the more active the animal is more rapidly it consumes its stored food. Warm blooded animals use up their stores of food in the body more quickly. A dog can survive without food for 20 days at the most. However, the bug is such a wonderful creature that it can survive without food for one full year.

But man cannot store food in his stomach. If he misses one meal, his condition becomes bad. Food is required to maintain the flow of blood. All the constituents of blood are obtained from food. The moment, the blood lacks nutritional materials, a signal, via blood, goes to the hunger centre of the brain and we start feeling hungry.

There are a few examples of persons who survived for a very long time without food. Angus Warviern of Scotland survived without taking any food for 382 days i.e. from June 1965 to July 1966. During this period, he took only coffee, tea, water and soda water. One South African woman survived for 102 days on water and soda water only. Stefan Taylor of New Zealand remained alive for 40 days in 1970 on a daily intake of one tumbler of water only. These are some uncommon examples. Such people are endowed with exceptional power. Common man can at the most survive without food for a week. OOO

103

5

What happens to our body in sleep?

Sleep is a bodily need that takes up about one third of life-span. After a whole day's toil, both brain and body get tired. Sleep is necessary to restore energy and freshness to the tired organs and tissues of our body. It enables the body to repair worn out tissues and cells.

Do you know how sleep comes to us and what happens to our body during sleep? According to scientific facts, there is a very complex area in the brain called "sleep centre". Calcium ions present in the blood, control this centre. When an optimum quantity of calcium is received by the "sleep centre", we get sleep. It has been observed from experiments on animals that they start sleeping when calcium is injected directly into the sleep centre. But if calcium is injected into the blood stream, this does not happen. During sleep, the sleep centre does two things. Firstly, it blocks off the brain so that we have no will-power or consciousness left and secondly, it blocks all nerves leading from the brain so that our internal organs and limbs fall asleep.

In sleep, our body continues doing many types of movements. A man on an average changes his sides 20 to 40 times during sleep in one night. Blood circulation continues during sleep. Heart beat slows down a little bit. The digestive system works normally. Liver and kidneys perform their functions. The effect of sound, light, heat, smell etc. in sleep are the same on every sleeping person. During sleep, the body temperature is lowered by about one degree centigrade and the body cells are quietly engaged in getting rid of waste materials that have accumulated during the active part of the day.

How many hours a healthy person should sleep? The number of sleeping hours needed varies with individuals. The average adult needs from 7 to 9 hours of sleep. Boys and girls of 15 years of age need about 10 hours sleep each night. It is wise to form the habit of going to bed at the same time each night. Insomnia is the condition in which a person has difficulty in falling asleep. Such sleeplessness is often associated with pain, but worry can also keep a person awake. A dark, quite room that is well ventilated and cool is good for sound sleep.　　OOO

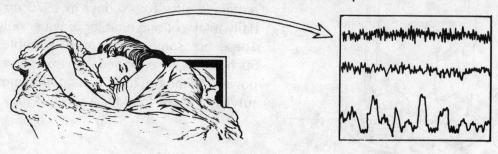

ECG recordings from a subject during different sleep phases

6

What causes people to faint?

We often see that people faint on hearing some sad news or on getting frightened suddenly. The bodies get drenched in sweat and become cold. Their faces turn pale. Physical consciousness diminishes. Unconsciousness can be caused not only by a shocking news or terrible fear, but by many other factors also. People may faint because of confinement in a close and poorly ventilated room, or because of hunger, fatigue, severe pain, emotional shock certain heart condition of sudden fall in blood sugar. Now the question arises: why do people become unconscious?

In order to know the reasons of fainting, it is essential to know what consciousness is. For the normal functioning of the brain, it is essential that there should be proper circulation of blood in the brain. As long as the brain is in receipt of proper supply of blood, all our physical activities remain normal. The normal functioning of the brain is in fact consciousness. If there is some obstruction in the supply of blood to the brain, the common physical processes get disturbed. Whatever may be the cause of fainting, man will become unconscious when normal supply of blood to the brain is disrupted. Hence, fainting or syncope is a temporary loss of unconsciousness resulting due to the insufficient supply of blood to the brain.

The state of unconsciousness can be prevented by some measures. If somebody feels that he is about to faint, he should immediately lie down. If that is not possible, he should bend downwards and enclose his head in between the knees. Both these measures enhance the blood supply to the brain and as soon as the brain starts receiving proper quantity of blood, the chances of one's becoming unconscious reduce.

If somebody has become unconscious, he should be laid down and his clothes should be loosened so that he can breathe easily. His head should be kept at a little lower level than rest of his body. This will increase the blood supply to his brain and he will regain consciousness. Once he is conscious, he should be given tea or coffee. If somebody has fainted because of head injury or heat stroke, he should be taken to the hospital immediately. ⭘⭘⭘

7

Why are people dwarf?

Generally most of the people are of normal height, but sometimes we come across people who are exceptionally tall or small. Persons who are exceptionally small are called dwarfs. In circus you must have seen such dwarfs who entertain you.

Do you know why some people lack normal height? The growth of a person depends on many factors. Heredity plays an important role in determining the height of a man or a woman. Children of tall parents are generally tall while of dwarf parents are dwarf. In Africa, some tribes such as the Watusi and the Masai have many men who are about 200 cm tall. At the same time, there are Pygmy tribes in Africa, whose people are only about 130 cm tall. These variations are due to heredity only.

Disease is also a reason causing dwarfness. There are cases of dwarfness in which head and trunk are normal in size, but arms and legs are short. This is caused by disease of cartilage. A normal body skeleton increases in length during childhood and adolescence because cartilage changes into bone at the growing ends of the bones. Disease of the cartilage prevents arms and legs from growing to a normal size.

Dwarfness is often caused by the lack of hormones produced by pituitary gland. The

Dwarf man

underactive pituitary gland during childhood does not allow the body to grow normally. This type of dwarfness can be treated by injecting hormones. Too much or too little growth is also determined by some disorder in adrenal, pituitary, thyroid and male and female sex glands (testes and ovaries). The growth retardation may also be due to inadequate nutrition and intake of vitamins. The restoration of an inadequate diet, vitamins and mineral intake will also cause the child's growth to spurt. A dwarf, named Jeffery Hudson, eighteen inches tall served as a captain of cavalry in the British Army. He lived from 1619 to 1692. OOO

8

How do we remember things ?

Memory can be defined as the capacity to keep information available for later use. The process of memory can be divided in to the four aspects — learning, retention and forgetting, and retrieval. The initial storage of information is called learning, keeping the new information available is called retention, the loss of new information over a period of time is called forgetting and utilization of stored information is called retrieval.

According to psychologists there are four kinds of learning. Classical conditioning is the simplest kind of learning. Ivan Pavlov studied it during the early 1900. He offered a dog food and at the same time rang a bell. The sight of food made the dog's mouth water. Pavlov called this an unconditioned response because it was not learned. Soon, however, ringing the bell was enough to cause the dog's mouth to water. This was called conditioned response. Classical conditioning is often called respondent learning.

Another form of learning is called instrumental learning. Often a person learns to do something as a result of what happens after the person does it.

Multiple response learning is the third type and it takes place when a skill is learned. A sequence of simple things must first be learned. Using a typewriter is our kind of multiple-response learning. At first, a person has to type letter by letter. With practice, the person learns to type word by word or phrase by phrase.

Fourth type of learning is insight learning. It means solving a problem through understanding how the different parts of a problem fit together. A simple example is that of a young child wanting to climb on the top of a table. The child may use a stool to get on to the chair and then use the chair to climb onto the table.

There are two basic theories to explain the process how we memorise events. According to one theory, memory is said to be stored in the brain as a memory trace. When we learn or experience something, impulses are generated in the nerves of the brain. These impulses impart their effects in the brain in the form of a record. According to the other theory, sensations created by learning produce some permanent changes in the brain

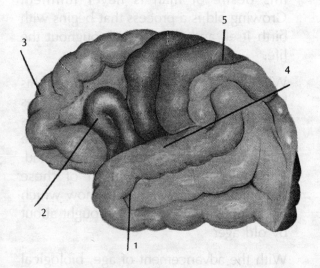

1. Memory, 2. Speech, 3. Thought, 4.Sight and hearing, 5. Sensory area

which remain there in the form of memory. According to some biologists, the R.N.A. (ribo-nucleic acid) present in the brain keeps the record of events. It has been observed that the quantity of R.N.A. present in the brain keeps on increasing from the age of three to the age of forty. During these years, the memory of the man also increases. The quantity of R.N.A. is almost constant from the age of 40 to 55 or 60. Therefore man's memory is almost consent during this period. After the age of 60, the quantity of R.N.A. starts decreasing and so does the memory.

The only effective way of remembering something is to repeat it many times. Interest is very important. Boring things are much more difficult to remember than something that we understand and are interested in. Motivation or desire to do something, is also important. ○○○

9

Why does man grow old ?

Every man in this world wishes to live long and nobody wants to grow old. But this desire of man is never fulfilled. Growing old is a process that begins with birth itself and continues throughout the life.

When the child is born, all the parts of his body are tiny. All the biological processes continue with a fast speed. As man grows older, biological changes take place in the body. These changes cannot be prevented. Old age is the culmination of these biological changes. Do you know which are the biological changes brought about by old age?

With the advancement of age, biological processes slow down, due to which the strength and sensitivity of man also diminish. This is because of the fact that the rate of production of proteins in the body decreases. Changes in the enzymes are also responsible for aging process. With reduced physical activity, man starts losing weight, his eye sight becomes weak and hair go grey. All these are the signs of the old age.

In old age, changes occur in all the cells and tissues of the body. The cells of kidneys, liver and intestines become weak. Blood vessels become old and consequently they are not able to carry blood and other nutrients adequately to all parts of the body. As a consequence aging increases. As the age advances, eyes, ears, skin, teeth and digestion become weak. Blood circulation becomes irregular. Finally life comes to an end.

The rate of growing old may be different with different people but old age spares none. This is a definite biological change which cannot be prevented. However, with the help of nutritional food, pure environment and proper exercises, early onset of old age can be prevented. ○○○

10

What causes baldness in people?

There are many theories regarding baldness. Some people treat baldness as the indication of the arrival of old age while some are of the view that bald men are intelligent. Baldness is also treated as a sign of richness. Some people think that bald men are fools. Whatever may be the significance of baldness, one thing is certain that by losing hair, man is deprived of his natural charm.

Baldness or alopecia is mainly of two types: permanent and temporary. Heredity, age and male sex hormone (androgens) production are three main factors causing permanent baldness. Other causes of permanent baldness are scar producing skin diseases, injuries, inborn lack of hair development and severe injury to hair growing centers caused by chemical or physical agents. Disease of the scalp is one important cause of baldness.

Temporary baldness may be due to high fever, typhoid, pneumonia, influenza etc. Hair start falling due to weakness also. Baldness caused by disease and weakness can be cured by nutritive diets and tonics. X-rays, ingestion of meals and drugs, malnutrition, skin disease and endocrine disorders are some other causes of temporary baldness.

Baldness can be controlled to some extent through proper care of hair and a balanced diet. No successful drug or therapy has yet been developed to treat baldness. Don't waste money on advertised patent medicines or so called, "cures"!   ○○○

Bald men

11

Why are vitamins essential for us?

Just as carbohydrates, proteins, fats, inorganic salts and water are the essential parts of our food, vitamins are also necessary to keep the body in good health. Lack or deficiency of vitamins can cause many disorders and diseases like loss in digestive power, weakening of eye-sight, general weakness, tiredness, dryness of skin, inflammation of gums, weakening of bones, beri-beri, rickets, etc.

What are vitamins? The word vitamin was coined in 1912 after the Latin word 'vita', which means life. In fact, vitamins are organic materials which are found in many food substances and are extremely essential for the proper functioning of the body. They are of many kinds and each vitamin has a separate role in keeping our body healthy. Twenty kinds of different vitamins have already been isolated, out of which six vitamins are most important. These are vitamins A, B, C, D, E, and K.

Vitamin A: Vitamin A is mainly found in milk, butter, cream, cheese, eggs, fish-oil, cabbage etc. It is very essential for the development of the body. Deficiency of vitamin A weakens eye sight and leads to night blindness. Vitamin A protects us from infections, skin diseases and many eye diseases.

Vitamin A is needed for a healthy skin and respiratory system, and also for the eyes.

Vitamin B helps the body to release energy and in the production of red blood cells.

Vitamin C makes a substance which binds body tissue together, and helps us resist germs.

Vitamin D builds strong bones and teeth. It is produced by skin exposed to sunlight and in some foods.s

Vitamin E is important for reproduction. It is present in most green vegetables.

Vitamin K is used to produce a substance.

Vitamin B Complex: Vitamin B consists of many water soluble vitamins of the same nomenclature. They are known by their chemical names. Their constitution and functions are also different. These are described below.

(i) Vitamin B$_1$ (Thiamine): Vitamin B$_1$ or thiamine is found in yeast, germinated wheat and pork. Its deficiency leads to a disease called beri-beri and causes tiredness, weakness, breathing difficulties, indigestion etc. Vitamin B$_1$ is lost if food is cooked with baking soda.

(ii) Vitamin B$_2$ (Riboflavin): Vitamin B$_2$ or riboflavin is mainly found in milk, egg and liver. Deficiency of Vitamin B$_2$ causes general weakness, skin diseases, wounds on tongues and cracks on lips. Eyes are also affected; there is dimness in vision, redness or burning sensation in the eyes.

(iii) Vitamin B$_6$ (Nicotinic Acid or Niacin): Vitamin B$_6$ or nicotonic acid or niacin is found in bigger proportion in yeast, grain chaffs, eggs, meat, kidneys and livers. This is also found in smaller quantities in flour, polished rice, fruits, green vegetables, and milk.

Deficiency of vitamin B$_6$ causes a disease called pellagra. This causes mental tension, inflammation of tongue, gums and inner lining of the intestine. There is loss of appetite and body becomes weak.

(iv) Vitamin B$_7$: Vitamin B$_7$ is found in eggs, meat, milk and green vegetables. Deficiency of this vitamin adversely affects the inner lining of stomach and intestines, thereby causing disorder in digestion.

(v) Vitamin B$_{12}$: Vitamin B$_{12}$ is found in milk, meat, liver etc. By keeping the diet balanced, it can be obtained in sufficient quantity. Deficiencies of this vitamin can result in anaemia, pains, toughness in arms, and partial paralysis. For the formation of red blood corpuscles, Vitamin B$_{12}$, Folic acid and Vitamin C are essential. In case of an extreme anaemic condition, it is injected into the body.

Vitamin C (Ascorbic Acid): Vitamin C or ascorbic acid is found in large quantities in orange, lemon, grape, tomatoe, pineapple, germinated pulses and green vegetables. Pears, plums, bananas also have it.

Deficiency of Vitamin C leads to pain in joints, and a disease called scurvy. Inflammation of gums, weakening of brain, lethargy, weakness, tiredness, pain in legs, loss of eyesight, appearance of blue scars on the body, and peeling of skin are also caused by its deficiency.

Vitamin D: Vitamin D is found in milk, butter, fish-oil, egg etc. The sunlight falling on the body also makes vitamin D inside the skin. Deficiency of this vitamin causes a disease called rickets (weakening of bones).

Vitamin E: Vitamin E is found in grains and oils. It is also found in a large quantity in onions. Deficiency of this vitamin badly affects skin, blood, brain and liver.

Vitamin K: Vitamin K is found in green leafy vegetables. Generally, the organisms present inside the intestines make vitamin K. It helps in clotting of blood on wounds.

If we take balanced diet containing fresh vegetables, fruits, eggs, milk, fish, beans wheat and rice, we get all these vitamins. All these vitamins are also available in the form of tablets and capsules in the market.

OOO

12

Why do we get fever?

The normal body temperature of a healthy man is 98.4°F (37°C). Fever is a condition in which the body temperature rises above the normal. It is a common symptom of disease.

The heat energy produced by the chemical reactions taking place inside the body is controlled by brain and skin. As long as there is no disease or malfunctioning in the body, the temperature remains 98.4°F. When germs of some specific disease attack the body, pyrogens are produced in the body cells. Consequently, the centres controlling the body temperature are affected and, as a result, body temperature starts rising. This rise in temperature is called fever. The first signs of fever are chills, loss of appetite and a feeling of weakness.

Fever is a body mechanism that helps us in destroying the germs of diseases. During fever, some of the body organs start working fast and some physiological processes get accelerated. The rate of production of hormones, enzymes and blood cells increase considerably. These hormones, enzymes and blood cells start fighting the germs causing fever. During fever, blood circulation and respiration become faster. Both these processes help the body in getting rid of the poisonous germs present in the body. Fevers are often the symptom of a serious infection.

There are various kinds of fever — malaria, typhoid, etc. Persistence of any fever for a longer period is not good. During fever, the internal parts become hot and there is deficiency of water causing the contraction of the capillaries of blood and urinary tracts. Protein accumulated in the body gets depleted. Disorder sets in the brain due to high temperature. It is, therefore, a big mistake on the part of anybody, if he or she ignores fever. Though fever is a physiological activity aimed at fighting any disease, it is extremely essential to seek immediate medical assistance once you get it.　OOO

13

How do bones mend?

A fracture is a break in a bone. Bones may break or fracture in several different ways. A simple fracture is one in which the two ends remain in position, and not much damage is done to the surrounding tissue. In a compound fracture, the broken bone sticks out through the skin. A comminuted fracture is a bone that has splintered or shattered. An impact fracture involves the ends of two bones rubbing each other. A greenstick is a partial break of a bone. In other kinds of fracture large blood vessels may be damaged or the bone ends may be smashed.

A fracture causes pain and inflammation in the area around it. Usually, when a fracture occurs, a doctor must set the bone right so that it may heal properly. A plaster cast is often applied to the limb with the fracture to assure proper healing.

The healing process begins when blood from broken blood vessels clots. After a few days the broken ends of the bone become soft and the space between them is filled with a sticky 'glue' which contains bone forming cells.

Within two or three weeks, new soft bone tissues completely fill the gap between the broken ends. They slowly harden. The

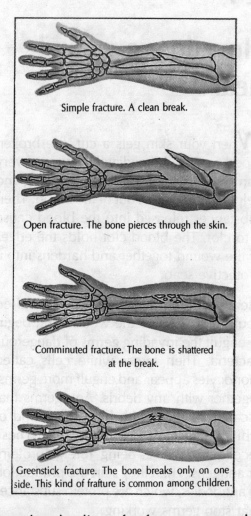

Simple fracture. A clean break.

Open fracture. The bone pierces through the skin.

Comminuted fracture. The bone is shattered at the break.

Greenstick fracture. The bone breaks only on one side. This kind of frafture is common among children.

complete healing of a fracture may take several months. The only necessary condition is that the two broken pieces must be held in place for several weeks so that they can grow together properly.

Older people with brittle bones are most apt to get a fracture. Children tend to resist fracture. ○○○

14

How does a wound heal?

When your skin gets a cut, the broken blood vessels immediately become very narrow. This stops excessive bleeding and helps to keep germs out of the blood. Then substances released into the blood cause it to clot. The blood clot holds the edges of the wound together and hardens into a protective scab.

Meanwhile white blood cells called neutrophils rush to the wound and begin to engulf the invading germs of dangerous bacteria. Then larger white cells called monocytes appear and engulf more germs, together with any debris. Any germs that escape are dealt with by a third kind of white cells called lymphocytes. These recognize germs as being 'foreign protein' or antigens. Then they start the production of antibodies, which are protein substances that stop germs working.

In the lower layer (the dermis) of the skin, special cells called fibroblasts move into the wound and start producing new tissues. These new tissues are essential for the healing of the wound. In the upper layer (epidermis), the cells around the wound start multiplying and filling the gap. When

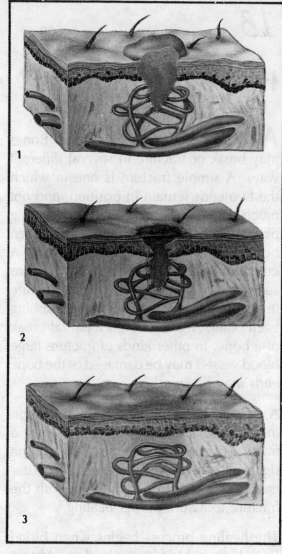

1. Blood coming from wound
2. Scab being formed to stop flow of blood
3. Wound heals after some time

the process of new skin tissue development beneath the scab is nearly complete, the scab falls off. In this way the wound gets healed. ○○○

114

15

Which of the body parts can be replaced with artificial parts?

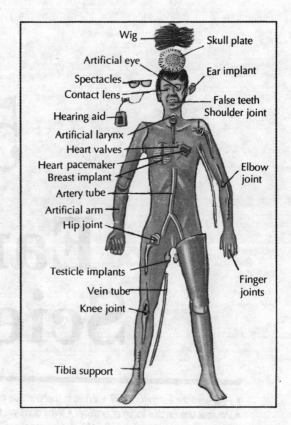

During the past two decades bio-engineers have developed a number of artificial substitutes for diseased tissues and organs. Some of these, such as, kidney dialyzers are external devices. Other such as plastic heart valves and artificial blood vessels are implanted inside the body, replacing the diseased or damaged ones. Two devices—the dialyzer and artificial heart valves are of special interest.

The artificial kidney or dialyzer performs the function of removing wastes from the blood of a person whose kidneys do not work properly. It is an external device and patient needs dialyses twice a week. With this machine a person can be kept alive for years.

In April 1969, Dr. Denton A. Cooley of St. Luke's Episcopal Hospital in Houston, placed a Dacron and silastic heart (artificial heart) into a dying man. Three days later a cadaver heart became available and was used to replace the artificial device. The next day the patient died. Some 13 years later, at the university of Utal medical centre, an artificial heart powered by a 170 kilogram external system, was implanted in the chest of 62 years old Barney Clark. He died 112 days later of multiple organ collapses. The heart was in perfect working condition.

In 1984-1985, several artificial heart implants were performed in the United States and Sweden. Good life spans have been achieved but against a tremendous cost.

Artificial teeth have been used by humans for a long time very successfully.

The heart, the lung, the liver, the kidney, the adrenal glands and cornea can be transplanted from one human being to another. Success rate of transplantations of human organs is much higher than that of artificial parts.   ○○○

5
Earth Science

• How was the Earth formed? • What is there inside the Earth? • How do we measure the mass of the Earth? • What is the Earth's force of gravity? • Why don't we feel the Earth's motion? • How many kinds of climate are there? • How seasons change? • What is atmosphere? • What is air and how is it useful for us? • Does air have weight? • How is the wind velocity measured? • How does it rain? • What is monsoon? • How are clouds formed? • What are tornadoes, hurricanes and cyclones? • How are hails formed? • How is fog formed? • What are lightning and thunder? • How were mountains formed? • How were rivers formed? • How are caves formed? • How are Volcanoes formed? • What causes an Earthquake? • How are lakes formed? • How are springs formed? • How are waterfalls formed? • What are glaciers? • Why is the sea water salty? • How were the oceans formed? • What is Dead Sea? • Are there mountains inside the sea?

1

How was the Earth formed?

Our Earth was born around 4.6 billion years ago. Like the Sun and other planets, it was also formed out of the clouds of dust and gases. However, before turning into present shape it was a fireball surrounded by an atmosphere of burning gases. At that time it revolved round the Sun in the form of a hot spherical body. Hundreds of years later, it gradually started moving away from the Sun while still revolving round it. As it moved farther and farther from the Sun, its temperature kept on decreasing. It started cooling off and its outer layer changed into a crust. With the hardening of this crust, cracks developed in it and molten material from inside started coming out. Over a period of millions of years, this molten material gave birth to mountains and valleys.

As time passed by, the thick layer of hot gases enveloping the Earth cooled off and turned into clouds. These clouds rained on the Earth for a long time. Rain-water accumulating in the low-lying areas of the Earth turned into the oceans. With the passage of time, there were upheavals due to which its surface was raised high or pressed down. This produced many volcanoes. Slowly it became calm and the seas and mountains took their definite shapes.

Subsequently, around 570 million years ago, micro-organisms started developing on the Earth. In the first 345 million years, marine (aquatic) animals came into existence. As more time passed, the aquatic animals also underwent changes.

In the next phase of evolution, the great reptiles — creatures crawling on the Earth — came into existence. And finally around a million years ago man was born through evolution.

Today, Earth has all the favourable conditions required for the existence of life. It has an atmosphere absolutely essential for the living beings. OOO

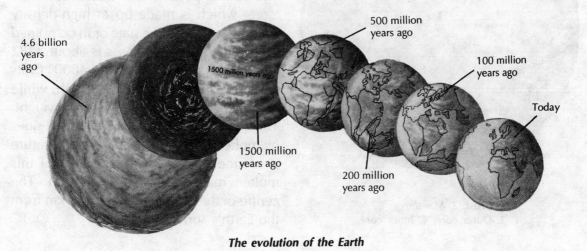

4.6 billion years ago

1500 million years ago

1500 million years ago

500 million years ago

200 million years ago

100 million years ago

Today

The evolution of the Earth

117

2

What is there inside the Earth?

Man has always been curious to know about the internal structure of the Earth. He tried digging and other direct methods and, finally, found out an indirect method to know the interior of the Earth—through the study of earthquake vibrations of Seismic waves. Studies reveal that our Earth has three main layers — the outer surface on which we live is called the 'Earth's crust', below it is the 'mantle' and then comes the 'core'.

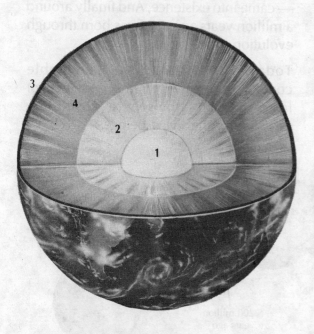

1. Crust, 2. Mantle,
3. Outer core, 4. Inner core

The outer layer or the Earth's crust, has two sub-layers — the first layer is the lighter one and is called Sima (for silica-magnesium) while the second sub-layer is heavier than the first and is called 'Sial' (for silica-aluminium). Thus, the Earth's crust is mainly composed of silica. Its depth varies from 16 km to 50 km on land and about 5 km under the oceans. The volume of this crust is only 1% of the Earth's volume, while its weight is around 4% of the Earth's total weight. As we go down the Earth's crust, the temperature increases. At every 35 metres in depth, there is an increase of about 1° C. At a depth of 3 km, the temperature is around 100° C (boiling point of water) and at 50 km, the temperature is 1,200° C—hot enough to melt rocks.

The next layer below the crust is called 'mantle'. It is 2,880 km thick. It is mainly composed of silicon magnesia and iron. The rocks in the mantle are denser than sial and sima. Its total volume is 84% of the Earth's volume. Its weight is around 67% of the Earth's weight.

The central portion of the Earth is called 'core' which is made up of high-density solid materials, in free state or in combined form in rocks. Its thickness is about 3482 km. Its temperature is around 4800° C. Its volume is 15% of that of the Earth, while its weight is 32% of the Earth's weight. This solid core is surrounded from all sides by molten iron and nickel. Its temperature is around 3900°C. The thickness of this molten mass is around 2,240 km. The centre of the Earth is some 6,336 km from the Earth's surface. ⊙⊙⊙

3

How do we measure the mass of the Earth?

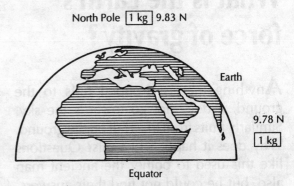

North Pole [1 kg] 9.83 N

Earth

9.78 N

[1 kg]

Equator

Mass never changes, but weight depends on the force of gravity. The Earth is not perfectly round; it is wider at the equator than the poles. So while at the North Pole 1 kg mass weighs 9.83 newtons (N), at the Equator it weighs 9.78 N

When we want to know the mass of a particular object we weigh it in a balance. The size of the balance varies with the size of the object to be weighed. But Earth is a giant body and to think of a balance for weighing it is almost impossible. Then, what is the way out? Scientists have simplified matters in this regard. Newton's law of gravitation is used to determine Earth's mass. According to this law, there exists a force of attraction between any two bodies of the universe and this is dependent on the masses of the two bodies as well as on the distance between them. The force of attraction is directly proportional to the product of the masses of the two bodies, and inversely proportional to the square of the distance between them.

An experiment is performed to determine Earth's mass with the help of the above mentioned law. In this experiment, a small metallic ball is suspended with the help of a thin thread. The position of this ball is accurately determined. Now a big lead-ball weighing a ton is brought near this ball. The small ball is attracted towards the big ball due to the gravitational pull and as such it is slightly displaced from its initial position in respect to the big ball. The change in the position of the small ball is even less than one-tenth of an inch. This displacement is very accurately measured with the help of the precision instruments. Using the value of this displacement in a formula of physics, the mass of the Earth is calculated. The mass of the Earth has been found to be 598× 10[19] (598,000,000,000,000,000,000,0) tons. ○○○

4

What is the Earth's force of gravity?

Anything that is dropped falls to the ground, it does not go towards the sky. Similarly fruits from trees fall on the ground. Why does it happen like this? Questions like this used to bother the ancient man also, but he could not find their answers. But today, it is an accepted fact that the Earth attracts everything towards its centre. That is why the fruits from trees or the ball thrown up, are all attracted towards the Earth. This invisible force of attraction between the Earth and any other body is called the force of gravity. The centre of gravity of the Earth lies in its centre. Imagine what would happen if a hole is drilled in the Earth from one side to the other, passing through its centre and a ball is dropped in this hole. The ball, in fact, will stop at the centre of Earth; it will not go to the other side. The weight of a body will be more, if it is nearer the centre of gravity of the Earth. Similarly the weight will be less if the body is away from it. This is why a body weighs more at the poles than at the equator, since the poles are nearer the centre than the places on the equator. Not only the Earth, but all other planets also have this force of gravity. As a matter of fact, every body in this universe attracts every other body with this force of gravitation and it is this force which keeps all the planets and stars suspended in the sky. It is this gravitational pull that keeps the moon revolving round the Earth and the Earth revolving round the sun. Naturally the moon also attracts the Earth and tides in the sea are mainly due to the gravitational pull of the moon.

Up to the end of the fifteenth century, it was assumed that if two bodies were simultaneously dropped from the same height in vacuum, the heavier body will hit the ground first. But this assumption was baseless. The famous scientist Galileo proved it in 1590 for the first time that irrespective of their masses, all the objects dropped simultaneously from the same point in a vacuum will reach the ground at the same time. From the Leaning Tower of Pisa, he dropped one ball of 100 pounds and another of just half pound at the same time and he demonstrated it in the presence of thousands of people that both the balls hit to the ground simultaneously.

Subsequently Newton propounded the law of gravitation. According to this law, the force of attraction between two bodies is directly proportional to the product of their masses and inversely proportional to the square of the distance between them. It follows from this that the force of attraction will be doubled if the mass of one of the two bodies is doubled. On the other hand if the distance between them is doubled, the force will be reduced to one-fourth of the initial value.

Scientists have not been able to fully explain the existence of the gravitational force of the Earth or of other heavenly bodies. The velocity of a freely falling body towards the Earth increases by 9.8 metres or 32 feet every second. This is called acceleration due to gravity. ooo

5

Why don't we feel the Earth's motion?

Till a few hundred years ago, it was believed that the Earth is the centre of the universe and that the Sun, the Moon and the stars revolve around it. This fact was based on the observation that the Earth is stationary while the position of stars is changing. In 1545, a Polish astronomer Copernicus suggested that the Earth revolves round the Sun. It was proved that it revolves round the Sun and completes one revolution in $365\frac{1}{4}$ days. This period is called a year. Secondly, it also rotates on its own axis and takes 24 hours to complete one rotation.

Naturally the question arises: if the Earth moves, why don't we feel its motion? The answer is: because of gravity, all the things situated on the Earth including the atmosphere move with the Earth and hence

we can't feel it is moving. You can understand this in a different way. If you rotate a football with an ant on it, the ant will not feel that the ball is rotating. Exactly like the ant on the football, we are situated on the surface of the Earth and we don't feel the movement of the Earth.

The biggest proof of the Earth's motion is the change in seasons. Seasons occur due to the Earth's motion round the Sun as well as due to its rotating on its own axis. Day and night are caused by the Earth's motion on its axis. The portion of the Earth which faces the sun experiences day while the remaining portion has night. If the Earth did not rotate on its axis, the part of the Earth facing the sun would always have had day while the rest would have had night for ever. The Earth's axis makes an angle of $23\frac{1}{2}°$ with the vertical. As such each pole faces the sun continuously for six months and for the next six months, it does not. This explains the six monthly duration of days and nights on the poles. All these observations confirm the motion of the Earth round the Sun as well as on its own axis. ooo

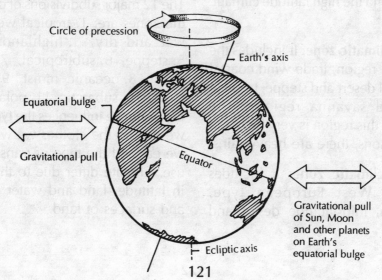

Circle of precession

Earth's axis

Equatorial bulge

Gravitational pull

Equator

Gravitational pull of Sun, Moon and other planets on Earth's equatorial bulge

Ecliptic axis

6

How many kinds of climate are there?

Climate is the average weather experienced by an area over a period of years. It depends upon the temperature, rains, atmospheric pressure, wind directions, mountains, height from the sea level and latitude of that place. Different kinds of climate are found in different parts of the world. Different instruments like thermometer, barometer, raingauge, etc. are used to study the climate, atmospheric pressure, wind directions, rains, clouds, humidity etc.

The world has been divided into 12 major climatic regions. For convenience, these climatic regions have been grouped into three on the basis of their latitudinal positions and extent. These are — the low latitude climatic zone, the mid-latitude climatic zone and the high latitude climatic zone.

Low latitude climatic zone: It includes the humid tropical region, trade wind coastal region, tropical desert and steppe, tropical monsoon and savanna regions. The temperature in this region is very high and dry. In all seasons, there are heavy rains.

Mid-latitude climatic zone: It includes China type. West European type, Mediterranean, mid-latitude desert and

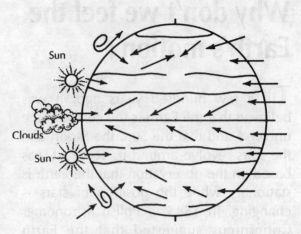

The position of the winds on Earth

steppe and Manhuria type climatic region. The summers are less hot, but the winters are very cold.

High latitude climatic zone: It includes Taiga type, Tundra type, ice-cap and high mountain type regions. In these places, temperature is very low during the winter and cold even during the summer.

The 12 major subdivisions of climate within the zones are: 1. tropical wet, 2. tropical wet and dry, 3. highlands, 4. desert, 5. steppe, 6. subtropical, 7. subtropical moist, 8. oceanic moist, 9. continental moist, 10. subarctic, 11. polar and 12. ice cap. Climate influences the types of houses we live in, the clothes we wear, the food we eat and the type of transportation we use. Climate differ due to the differences in latitude, land and water temperatures and surfaces of land. ○○○

7

How seasons change?

We know that the Earth revolves round the Sun and also rotates on its own axis. Days and nights are caused by the rotation of the Earth on its axis. The axis of the Earth makes an angle of $23\frac{1}{2}°$ with the vertical. It is this inclination which causes changes in seasons. With its inclined axis, when the Earth revolves round the Sun, the Sun rays make different angles at the same place at different times. Due to the variations in angles, the distribution of the solar heat is not the same at the same place. This uneven distribution of solar heat on the Earth leads to the summer or winter season.

If we look at the picture, we see that in June, when the northern hemisphere is tilted towards the Sun, it is summer in Europe, Asia and North America (northern hemisphere) and winter in the southern hemisphere. Six months later, in December, the southern hemisphere is tilted towards the Sun, so it is summer in southern hemisphere but winter in northern hemisphere.

On 21st March and 23rd September every year, the Sun is exactly over the equator. On these two days, the duration of the day and the night is the same (12 hours) at every place on the Earth. From 21st March to 21st June, the Sun advances from the equator to the Tropic of Cancer. This results in hot season in the northern hemisphere, where days become longer and nights

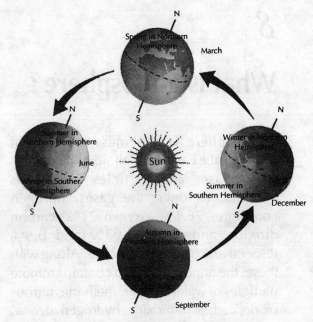

Earth's revolution around the Sun and rotation on its own axis change the seasons

shorter. During this period, it is winter in the southern hemisphere. From 21st June to 22nd December, the Sun advances towards the tropic of capricon. This causes the summer season in the southern hemisphere and winter in the northern hemisphere. In the northern hemisphere, the days are shorter and the nights are longer during this period. After 22nd December, the Sun again starts moving towards the north and reaches the equator again on 21st March. During this period, the days in northern hemisphere start getting longer and the nights shorter.

In March and September the Sun is overhead at the equater. Both hemispheres are enjoying either autumn or spring.

Thus, the revolution of the Earth round the Sun and its rotation on its own inclined axis changes the seasons as well as the duration of the days and the nights. ⊙⊙⊙

8

What is atmosphere?

Atmosphere is the mass of air that envelops the Earth from all sides. It contains many gases and particles of various material. Amongst the gases, nitrogen constitutes 78.1%, oxygen 21%, carbon dioxide and argon 0.03% and 0.9% respectively of the atmosphere. Along with these, the atmosphere also contains minute particles of water vapour, methane, nitrous oxide, carbon monoxide, hydrogen, ozone, helium, neon, krypton and xenon gases. In addition, sand-particles, smoke, salt-particles, volcanic ash-particles, meteoric dust and pollen are also present in the atmosphere.

The atmosphere is quite dense near the Earth's surface, but becomes rarefied as one goes above it. It is estimated that the atmosphere extends up to a height of 1,000 km.

It is made up of many layers. The pressure, density and temperature of the atmosphere vary with its distance from the Earth. At a height of 6 km, the air pressure is reduced to half of what it is at the Earth's surface. Similarly, the temperature falls by 1°F for every 91 metres.

On the basis of its physical properties, the atmosphere has been divided into the following five layers:

1. Troposphere: Troposphere extends from the Earth's surface to a height of 17 km. It accounts for 75% of the total weight of the

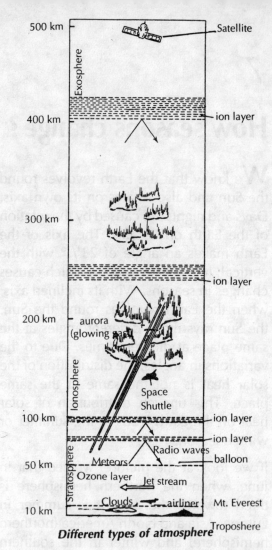

Different types of atmosphere

atmosphere. Almost all the living beings live in this part. As one goes up, the temperature decreases and becomes the minimum at a height of 10 km. Rains, clouds, storms and snow form in this very part. This is the most important atmospheric layer for living beings.

2. Stratosphere: Stratosphere extends up to a height of 48 km. Its upper portion contains ozone which absorbs ultra-violet rays coming from the sun. These rays are very dangerous for life. There are neither strong winds nor varying temperatures in this part. ○○○

3. Mesosphere: Mesosphere starts after a height of 50 km. Here the temperature is considerably low and it is the minimum at a height of 85 km.

4. Ionosphere: Atmospheric layer above the mesosphere and up to a height of about 500 km is called Ionosphere. It contains only charged particles. These charged particles reflect radio waves towards the Earth and make radio communication possible.

5. Exosphere: It is the outermost layer of the atmosphere. In this, the density of the atmosphere is very low. This part contains helium and hydrogen. So, the temperature is very high here.

The atmosphere is extremely useful for life. Without it we cannot survive. It protects us from the dangerous radiations of the Sun. The meteors also get destroyed after getting burned due to the atmospheric friction. OOO

9

What is air and how is it useful for us?

Air envelopes the entire surface of Earth. It is invisible, tasteless and has no smell. Air extends great distances above the Earth. One half of the air, by weight, is within 5.63 km of the earth's surface. The other half is spread over hundreds of kilometres beyond that.

Air is essential for life. No living being—plant or animal—can survive without it. It gives us energy and plants get their food from the carbon dioxide present in it.

What is air? It is a mixture of various gases—oxygen, nitrogen, carbon dioxide, inert gases (helium, neon, argon etc.) and water vapours etc. It contains 78% nitrogen, 21% oxygen, and 1% other gases.

First of all, oxygen helps in burning. If

there is no oxygen in the air, nothing will burn. Nitrogen, too, is a very useful gas. Molecular nitrogen is inert because of the strong triple bond between the two atoms, but it will react with some elements, especially the alkaline-earth metals, to give nitrides; with oxygen, and hydrogen. On the other hand, activated nitrogen, formed in an electric discharge, consists of nitrogen atoms and is much more reactive. Nitrogen compounds in the form of fertilisers are very useful for trees and plants. Carbon dioxide is used by plants for breathing. The water vapours in the air help to produce rain. The quantity of water vapour in the air varies from place to place. It determines the amount of rainfall at a place.

As we go up the Earth's surface, the pressure of the air decreases. The atmospheric pressure at the mountains is less because the molecules of air are separated from each other by larger distances. Therefore air is light there. This is why mountaineers need extra oxygen for breathing and carry oxygen cylinders with them. OOO

10

Does air have weight?

The Earth we live on is enveloped on all sides by air. Air is a gaseous state of matter. It is a mixture of nitrogen, oxygen, carbon dioxide, dust particles, water vapours, etc. which are all made up of molecules. That means, air is a mixture of molecules of many kinds. We know that molecules have their own weight and therefore air which is composed of all these molecules, also has weight.

This fact can be proved by a simple experiment. Take an empty football bladder and a small cord to tie around its neck. Weigh the bladder and the cord in a balance. Now fill the bladder with air and tie its neck with the cord and weigh it again, it weighs more than it weighed when it was empty. Thus, increase in the weight of the bladder is due to the air filled in it. This proves that air has weight. At sea level 0.03 cu m (1 cu ft) of air weighs 0.037 kg.

Because of the weight of air, the atmosphere exerts pressure on every object. This pressure is about 1 kg per sq. cm. Our palm measuring nearly 80 sq. cm experiences a force of 82 kg. If we calculate the total force exerted by it on our body, we find that it is more than the weight of three elephants. We do not feel it because our bodies are supported by equal pressure on the inside of our bodies.

On mountain tops, this pressure is very low. This is because air pressure decreases with the increase in height. But the pressure (inside the body) remains the same at those heights. If the atmospheric pressure is very low as compared to the blood pressure, blood can burst out of nose or ears.

OOO

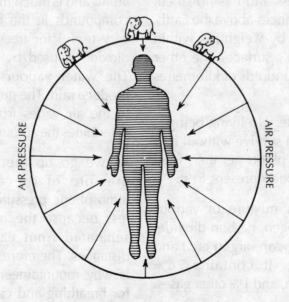

AIR PRESSURE

AIR PRESSURE

11

How is the wind velocity measured?

Wind is moving air. Slow winds are gentle breezes. Fast winds are gales. You can see the speed of the wind by its effect on trees and buildings, but can not measure it because it is invisible.

Tthe instrument used for measuring the velocity of wind is called the 'anemometer' or wind-gauge. It was invented by the English scientist Robert Hooke in 1667. There are many kinds of anemometers. Most of them consist of three or four small aluminium cups attached to an axle. These cups can freely rotate on being struck by winds. The higher the velocity of the wind, the faster is the speed of rotation of these cups. The rate of rotation of these cups in a fixed time is used to calculate the velocity of wind. This instrument has a meter whose pointer gives the speed of rotation of the cups. This meter is so calibrated that it directly gives the velocity of the wind.

Yóu might be wondering why it is necessary to measure the velocity of wind. When man started flying in aeroplanes, it became essential for him to know the wind's velocity. Initially he used to measure it by flying balloons in the sky, but with

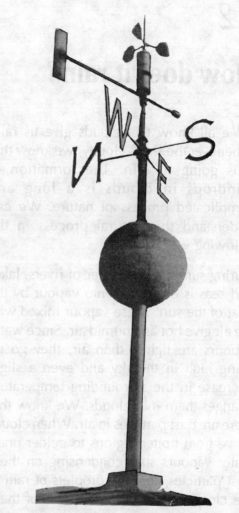

A transmitting cup anemometer, with wind vane

the invention of anemometers, it became easier. Scientists have succeeded in developing small anemometers of the size of 10 to 12 cm. Knowledge of the velocity of wind has proved very useful in meteorological studies especially in weather forecasting. Sailors also need to know the speed of wind.   ooo

12

How does it rain ?

We all know that clouds give us rain. Whenever the sky is cloudy, we know that it is going to rain. The formation of raindrops in clouds is a long and complicated process of nature. We can understand this natural process in the following way.

During summer, the water of rivers, lakes and seas is converted into vapour by the heat of the sun. These vapour mixed with the air give hot and humid air. Since water vapours are lighter than air, they go on rising high in the sky and even a slight decrease in the surrounding temperature changes them into clouds. We know that there are dust particles in air. When clouds move from hotter regions to colder ones, water vapours start condensing on these dust particles, forming droplets of rain in the clouds. Only when the size of these droplets increases due to further

condensation, they start falling down on the Earth due to the force of gravity, and we say that it is raining.

Thus for rains, it is essential that hot and humid air should be lifted up so that water vapour get condensed. Lifting of air takes place in several ways such as orographic lifting, frontal lifting and convectional lifting. Orographic lifting occurs when air is forced upwards by a natural barrier, like a mountain. In frontal lifting cool air of one air mass pushes beneath the warm air of the other air mass. Convectional lifting occurs due to the heat of the sun. Do you know that the highest rainfall of the world is at Cherapunji (Assam) in India? The average annual rainfall of this place is 1,200 cm. In 1861 the total rainfall recorded here was 2,175 cm.

In colder regions, condensation of water vapour takes place not only on the dust particles, but also on the small particles of ice formed in the clouds. Condensation also takes place on ions produced by lightning in the air. Water condensed on ice particles also falls down on the Earth in the form of rains. OOO

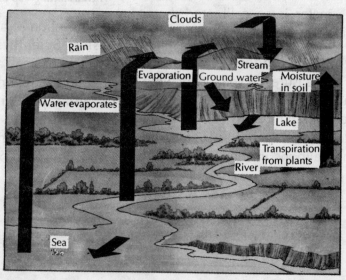

Cycle of water

13

What is monsoon?

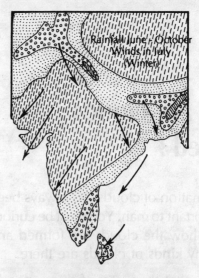

The word 'monsoon' is derived from the Arabic word 'mausim' meaning a season. It is a seasonal wind of South Asia blowing in summer from the ocean towards the land and in winter from the land to the ocean.

In South Asia, the wind from the Indian Ocean blowing towards the shore is the monsoon wind. This wind indicates the chances of rain. Monsoon is of two kinds: (i) southwestern or summer monsoon, and (ii) northeastern or winter monsoon. India gets 90% of its total rainfall from the summer monsoon. These winds advance from the Indian Ocean towards the shore in mid June and, after being obstructed by the Himalayas, cause rains in the plains. Contrary to this, in Central Asia and north India, very cold, dry and strong winds blow off-shore in winter. They are called winter monsoon or the retreating monsoon. They cause some rain in the coastal areas.

It is interesting to see how monsoon winds change the coastal weather. It is a scientific truth that big sub-continents warm up or cool off much faster than the seas adjoining them. The areas of central and south Asia start warming up in the spring and by summer they become very hot in comparison to the Indian Ocean in the south and the Pacific Ocean in the east. Due to the high temperature, there is a reduction in the air pressure on the land and, consequently, winds start blowing

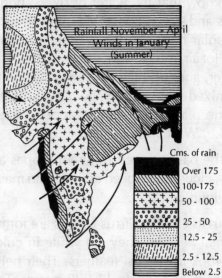

Cms. of rain	
	Over 175
	100-175
	50 - 100
	25 - 50
	12.5 - 25
	2.5 - 12.5
	Below 2.5

Summer monsoon brought by the Indian Ocean

from the sea to the shore. This is the summer monsoon. With the onset of the autumn, the entire Asia starts cooling fast and by the start of winter, the temperature is much less than that of the adjoining oceans. This increases the atmospheric pressure and, as such, in the winter, monsoon winds start blowing from the dry shore to the seas. The south and east Asia have a monsoon climate because of their large areas of land. ○○○

14

How are clouds formed?

The formation of clouds has always been very important to man. You must be curious to know how the clouds are formed and how many kinds of clouds are there.

We know that the water of rivers, ponds, lakes and seas is converted into vapour by the solar heat and this vapour moves in air. Hot air, mixed with water vapour, being lighter, goes up high in the sky. When the air mixed with water vapour accumulates at one place, it gives the appearance of smoke. We call it a cloud.

On the basis of their different shapes and sizes, clouds have been divided into mainly four kinds:

1. Cirrus clouds: Cirrus clouds are formed at great heights. They are white in colour and look like birds' feathers. Their height ranges from 8,000 to 11,000 metres. They are made up of small ice particles.

2. Stratus clouds: Stratus clouds are formed at a height of about 2,438 metres. They look like layers of fog. They foretell bad weather and drizzle.

3. Cumulus clouds: Cumulus clouds are formed at a height of 1,219 to 1,524 metres. They are dome-shaped at the top and flat at the bottom. They look like white mountains in the sky.

4. Nimbostratus clouds: Nimbostratus clouds are formed at the lowest heights. They are deep brown or black in colour. These are the clouds which rain.

There are ten different types of clouds. But the four discussed above are the main kinds.

If the air below clouds carrying condensed water vapour is cool, the size of the water droplets present in the clouds will go on increasing and when they attain an optimum size, they fall down on the Earth in the form of rain.

Similarly, if the air below these clouds is not cold, the water droplets present in the clouds will be reconverted into vapour. Consequently the clouds will disappear without raining. That is why some clouds disappear without raining.   OOO

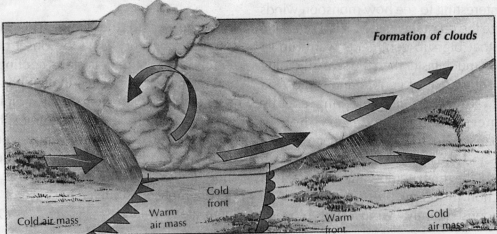

Formation of clouds

Cold air mass   Warm air mass   Cold front   Warm front   Cold air mass

15

What are tornadoes, hurricanes and cyclones?

Tornado

When wind moves with great speed and creates disturbance in the atmosphere, it is called a storm. Storms of summer are mainly caused by the rise in atmospheric temperature. Due to high temperature, air expands and there is a fall in the atmospheric pressure in that area. To balance it, air from colder regions where there is more pressure, rushes to the hotter regions. Carrying with it a large amount of dust and we call it a dust-storm.

Tornadoes, cyclones and hurricanes are some of the dangerous storms in which wind makes fast whirling motion. When the temperature of a small area rises to a high degree and, consequently, the atmospheric pressure falls, air from surrounding areas rushes in to fill this vacuum. Because of its fast velocity, wind's motion in that area becomes whirling. The hot air goes up fast, forming a funnel-shaped cloud. This is called a tornado. The pressure inside a tornado is so low that any object coming in its way gets sucked in. Wind velocity of a tornado goes up to 200 kilometres per hour.

Hurricanes generally belong to tropical areas. They engulf areas within a radius of 80 to 320 kilometers and the wind-speed goes up to 120 to 200 km per hour. The central portion of the hurricane extending from 5 to 15 kilometers, is completely calm. This is called the eye of the hurricane. When this portion reaches a particular area the air there comes to a standstill. This gives the impression that the hurricane is over. But, as soon as it leaves the area, it is followed by strong gusts of wind. Since hurricane also is a kind of whirling storm, it advances with a very fast whirling motion. It is called typhoon in east India and in the areas adjoining the Chinese Sea.

The cyclone is also a very dangerous storm. It devastates very large areas. It is caused by the rush of air towards low-pressure areas resulting in large-scale destruction. The violent cyclone which hit East Pakistan (now Bangladesh) on November 13–14, 1970 claimed lives of one million people.

○○○

16

How are hails formed?

Occasionally, you must have seen, some round balls of ice accompanying heavy rains. These round balls are called hails. They are seen more often in summer than in winter. Hailstones are of varying sizes. You may be curious to know how hails are formed in the atmosphere!

When raindrops start falling from the clouds towards the Earth, sometimes they have to pass through very cold regions and due to this low temperature, these raindrops get frozen. These frozen raindrops are called snow flakes. Sometimes these snow flakes are lifted up by strong winds to regions already having raindrops. As a consequence they get stuck to these snow flakes. When they fall through colder regions of the atmosphere,

they are again frozen. This way the size of the frozen raindrops goes on increasing. When the weight of these frozen drops is more than the upthrust of the air, they fall down on the Earth in the form of hailstones.

If you cut a hailstone into slices, you will notice many layers of transparent and semi-transparent snow. These layers are formed by the repeated freezing of the water-drops. The diameter of hailstones varies from 1 cm to 8 cm. A hailstone may weigh even more than half a kilogram. On 6 July, 1928, a very big hailstone fell at a place named Potter, Nebraska. It weighed 717 gm and had a diameter of 15 cm.

Hailstones can cause extensive damage. It has been observed that some animals and human beings have even succumbed to the injuries caused by hailstones. Hailstones are very damaging to the crops—they destroy the standing crops. On 30th April 1886, 246 people died of injuries caused by hailstones in Moradabad in UP (India). ooo

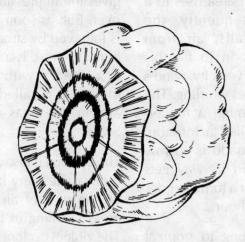

The cross-section of hailstone shows its layers

132

17

How is fog formed ?

During winter mornings, sometimes we see a smoky cover on the Earth's surface. This is called fog. When becomes very dense, the visibility is poor, and it becomes difficult to see anything.

Fog is a kind of cloud, which comes in contact with the ground. It is formed by the condensation of water vapour present in the air near the ground. We know that water vapour are always present in air. Air cannot hold more than a certain amount of water vapour at a given temperature. The water vapours in excess of that limit are converted into small particles of water or ice. When such condensation takes place near the Earth's surface, a cloud of fog is formed. The minute particles of water present in the fog reduce visibility to a great extent. During winter, the Earth's surface is cool in the mornings, as such, water vapour present in the air condense into fog.

The layers of fog are thicker in big cities than in villages and smaller towns. This is so because there is a greater degree of dust particles and smoke in big cities. Dust particles and smoke get mixed with water particles present in the fog and make it more dense. This type of fog is also called smog. You must have noticed that fogs are denser in those cities where there is more of smoke due to the large number of factories. In big industrial cities like Bombay, Calcutta and Delhi, this type of dense fog is a common feature.

The presence of fog causes a great inconvenience to the transport system. Sometimes, planes and motor cars meet with accidents because of the poor visibility due to fog. In 1955, a chemical method was developed to clear the fog. In this method, silver iodide or calcium chloride is sprayed in foggy areas which enables water particles present in the fog to fall down on the Earth in the form of raindrops. However, no system has succeeded fully in cleanring fog so far. ooo

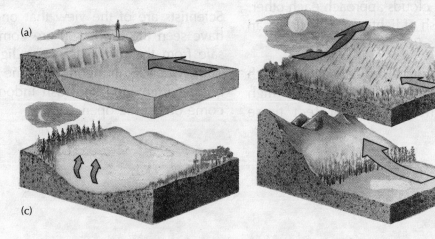

a) Advoction fog, b) Frontal fog, c) Radiation fog, d) Upslope fog

133

18

What are lightning and thunder?

Rain is often accompanied with thunder and lightning. Even though lightning and thunder are simultaneously produced in the clouds, the flash of lightning reaches us much before the sound. This is because light travels much faster than sound.

Although lighting seldom reaches the Earth, there have been instances of death by lightning. When it flashes, a bright streak is drawn in the clouds. In reality, this streak is there either between two clouds or between the clouds and the Earth. Whenever a charged cloud approaches the Earth's surface, opposite charge is produced in it. When the potential difference between the two is much higher than the resistance of the air, electricity flows through the air towards the Earth. As a result, lightning flashes. Similarly, when two charged clouds approach each other, there is a flash of lightning. This flash can be as long as 50 km.

The lightning produced between the Earth and the clouds, is dangerous for high buildings. In order to protect these

Lightning

buildings from lightning, pointed metallic rods are fixed at the roof-tops of these buildings and these rods are taken through the walls down to the Earth and buried in it. They are called lightning conductors. Buildings fitted with these conductors cannot be damaged by lightning.

Scientists are of the view that once you have seen the flash, you are completely safe from the ill-effects of the lightning. Thus, when lightning flashes, one should not get frightened and rush indoors, but come out in the open.   ○○○

19

How were mountains formed ?

A mountain is a tract of land rising considerably above the surrounding surface. Mountains are usually found connected in chains or ranges.

Geologists have made extensive study of mountain formations. It has been revealed by these studies that they are formed as ranges. The ranges of mountains alongwith many small and big hills extend over long distances. To study their formation in a systematic way, geologists have divided them into four categories. Different types of mountains are formed in different ways. But all the mountains have been formed due to the violent changes on the Earth's surface, millions of years ago. The formation of four types of mountains can be understood in the following way.

The first type of mountains is the **volcanic mountains.** These mountains are made of lava and ash. Due to the agitations in the Earth's interior, the Earth's surface breaks at places from where the internal matter of the Earth comes out as lava. The volcanic mountains are cone-shaped with a large hole or crater at the top. The Vasuvius of Italy, the Fujiyama of Japan, the Hood and the Ranier of the United States of America are the famous volcanic mountains of the world.

The second type of mountains is the **folded mountains.** These are made of many layers of rocks. These layers are formed because of extreme contractions and pressures inside the Earth. The Alps mountain ranges have been formed in this way.

The third type of mountains is the dome-shaped and hence it is called **dome mountains.** When molten lava comes out of the earth with great pressure, it cools off in the form of a dome and, as a result, dome mountains are formed. The Black Hills of South Dakota are the examples of the dome mountains.

The fourth type of mountains is called **block mountains.** These are formed due to the occurrence of faults in the layers of the Earth. Sometimes there are such great upheavals inside the Earth that whole blocks of rocks from inside the Earth come

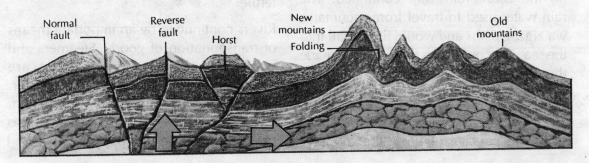

Formation of Mountains

135

up and constitute the block mountains. The Sierra Nevada Range of California in the United States of America is an example of the block mountains. Its one block is 640 km long and 128 km wide.

The rate of increase in the height of mountains is as low as a few millimetre per year.

However, with the passage of time, mountains get destroyed too. Rains, storms, and the flowing water coming from molten ice go on eroding small parts of the soil and rocks of mountains. As a result of this process, even big mountains are converted into small hills or plains in due course of time. ooo

20

How were rivers formed ?

The word river is derived from the Latin word 'ripa' meaning river bank. In the ancient times, a stream of water with definite banks was called a river. According to contemporary definitions, giant streams of water without any definite banks are called rivers. Smaller streams of water are known as brooks.

In the beginning of the creation of the universe, when mountains and seas formed on the Earth, rains still continued. The rain-water used to travel from mountains via zigzag paths and would finally fall into the sea. The continuous flow of water made these tracks deeper and wider. These streams of water underwent many changes and subsequently became rivers.

With the passage of time, the forms of rivers have changed. Now most of the rivers originate from mountains. The water in these rivers is molten snow coming down from heights. Rains also contribute to the water flowing in the rivers.

Some rivers are formed by the movement of glaciers. The uneven areas coming in the way of glaciers become plain and take the shape of a river. Sources of some of the rivers are springs and lakes. A river flows very slowly near its origin, but as it advances, its depth reduces and its banks become wide because of soil erosion. A river becomes very slow at its fag end. There is enough accumulation of soil at the point where a river meets the sea or a lake and the place where they meet is called a delta. Those areas where a river deposits silt brought by it become very fertile.

Rivers continue to be an important means of transportation of goods. Steamers and boats are plied in rivers. Dams are constructed in rivers to accumulate water, and, by making water fall from a height, electricity is generated. This water is also used for irrigation purposes. ooo

21

How are caves formed?

Caves have for long been linked with the history of civilisation in many interesting ways. In the stone age, men used to live in caves to protect themselves from cold and animals. Ancient people had many strange notions about caves. The people of Greece believed that their gods Zeus, Pan, Dionsus and Pluto lived· in caves. The Romans believed that caves were the homes of nymphs and sibyls. People of Persia worshipped caves considering them to be the abodes of God. Today, huge and beautiful caves all over the world have become centres of attraction for the tourists. Do you know how these caves were formed?

A cave is a deep hollow space in a mountain. It is formed in different ways.When water waves coming from the sea, collide with the mountains, they wash away the soft stones present in between the layers of the rocks. This process continued over a period of thousands of years and created large spaces inside the mountains which we call caves.

Some caves are found below the Earth's surface also. These have been formed by the water streams flowing below the Earth's surface. The underground water streams wash away the lime-stone from the rocks and the voids so created are called caves.

The sea-waves wash away the stones from the mountains forming the caves

Quite often, waterfalls create hollow spaces within the rocks which ultimately become caves. Such caves have been formed below the Niagara Falls.

Caves are also formed by the volcanic changes taking place in the earth's layers. Some caves are very long while some are very deep. The deepest cave is 'Guffre de la piere st.' situated on the border of France and Spain. It is 1310 metres (4300 ft) deep. The longest cave, 'Flit Ridge cave system' is situated in America and is 116.8 km (73 miles) long.

The longest single cavern in the world is the Sarawak chamber in Eastern Malaysia. It is 700 metres long and was discovered in 1980. Mammoth Cave National Park in the US State of Kentucky is the largest cave system of the world about 307 km long. In India, caves of Ajanta and Ellora are famous for their beautiful sculptures.

○○○

22

How are Volcanoes formed?

A volcano is a mountain having an opening on the surface of the Earth from which fire, smoke and ashes come out continuously. Mountains of this type are created by upheavals inside the Earth.

The formation of volcanoes can be understood as follows. Temperature inside the Earth goes on increasing as we go into the interior of the Earth. At a depth of approximately 30 km, the temperature is so high that it can melt rocks. When rocks inside the Earth get melted, they start expanding. These molten rocks are known as magma. In some parts of the Earth, this magma starts coming up through openings in the Earth's crust. When the pressure exerted by this magma is considerably high

and the Earth's crust at some places is weak, the crust breaks at those places and, as a result, hot gases, liquid and solid material of the red molten rocks start coming out. This is called volcanic eruption. The ejected hot smoke, ashes and stone pieces constitute what we call lava. This lava goes on solidifying in the shape of a cone and, on cooling, it takes the form of a mountain on the surface of the Earth.

Fire and smoke keep on flowing out of the opening of the volcano until the molten material inside the Earth is exhausted. Such volcanoes from which lava stops coming are called dead volcanoes. There are more than 450 volcanoes in the world. The number of volcanoes in Indonesia is quite large. The highest dead volcano of the world is in Argentina; it is 6,960 metres high. One of the most violent volcanic eruption was on the island of Krakatoa, near Sumatra in 1883 which produced tidal waves in the oceans throughout the world. ○○○

Various stages of active volcanoes

23

What causes an Earthquake?

Earthquakes are common occurrences. We often read about them in newspapers or listen over the radio. Do you know how they are caused?

When an earthquake occurs, that particular part of the Earth experiences tremors. Sometimes it is so mild that it passes unnoticed. But, often, it is quite strong and creates vast openings in the Earth's surface—buildings fall down and many lives are lost.

Destruction caused by the earthquake

We know that the Earth's surface is composed of various kinds of high and low rocks. Due to the internal upheavals of the Earth or the uneven pressure, malformation sets in the rocks. Due to the excessive pressure, the layers of rocks crack suddenly. After breaking, they either go up or down inside the Earth. At the places where such changes take place in the rocks, the Earth's crust experiences big shocks. These shocks cause vibrations which spread through the Earth's surface. All those areas through which these vibrations travel are said to be affected by an earthquake and, as a result of these vibrations, buildings fall down and lives are lost. The point of origin of an earthquake is called the epicentre of the earthquake.

Some places on the Earth are prone to earthquakes. Japan has the highest incidence of earthquakes. The Earth surface in Japan is uneven throughout and so the occurrence of earthquakes is very common there.

San Francisco, Lisbon, China, India and Japan have all suffered great loss of lives and property from the occurence of earthquakes.

Scientists have developed an instrument called the seismograph to study earthquakes. This instrument has arrangements to study the seismic waves caused by the earthquakes. Seismographs have been installed at various places in the world to record the seismic vibrations with a view to help mankind from the dangers of earthquakes. But it is impossible to forecast an earthquake or prevent it from happening.   ○○○

24

How are lakes formed?

Lakes are large masses of water formed mainly in low-lying areas of the Earth. Their main sources are rain-water or molten snow or, at times, a small river or a stream. Do you know how these lakes are formed?

Lakes are formed in many ways. Some lakes lie in the natural hollow of an old volcano. For example, the **crater lake** of Oregon in South America. Due to some upheavals, like falling of a meteor large ditches were formed on the surface of the earth, which later got filled with rain water — for example, Lake Bosuntui in Ashanti crater in Ghana.

The **Glacial lakes** are formed because the sliding glaciers cause big ditches on the Earth's surface which become lakes after rain-water and molten snow accumulate there. The Winnipeg Lake of Canada was formed by glaciers.

Rift valley lakes are formed when Earth's crust slips down between long lines of faults, the water fills part of the floor of the valley e.g. Lake Malawi and and Lake Turkana in East Africa.

Artificial lakes are created when people make dams to hold back river water.

While water of some lakes is saline, it is sweet in some others. The lakes from which water does not flow out, have saline water whereas the lakes into which some rivers fall or from which rivers originate have sweet and fresh water. The Superior Lake of America has sweet water.

There are innumerable lakes in the world. The Ojera Baikal Lake of central Asia is the deepest lake. It has 22,000 cubic km. water. It is 620 km. long and about 115 km. wide. Its depth is 2,400 metres. The Superior Lake of America has 12,000 cubic km. water. Seventy percent of the world's lakes are situated in Africa, Asia and North America. ○○○

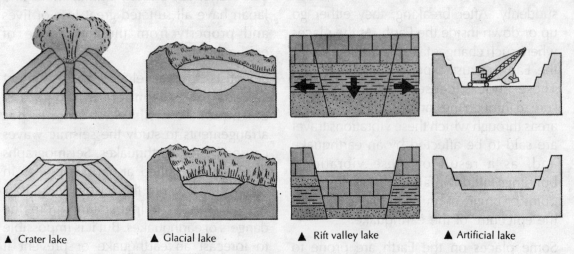

▲ Crater lake ▲ Glacial lake ▲ Rift valley lake ▲ Artificial lake

Types of lakes

25

How are springs formed?

Sometimes a stream of water suddenly bursts out from an opening in the Earth in the form of a fountain. This is called a spring. Springs generally erupt out of rocks. Springs are of cold water usually but some are hot springs or sulphur springs.

When it rains, the Earth absorbs a part of the rain-water while the remaining water gets evaporated. Due to the Earth's gravitational force, the water so absorbed keeps on going down through the holes and cracks in the Earth. And, when this water encounters some rocks on the way, it accumulates there. When this accumulated water finds an opening to come out, it bursts out as a spring. They are often found where permeable rocks lie above impermeable one, particularly in low lying areas.

Sometimes the water accumulated inside the Earth has to pass through sections containing sulphur and lime. The sulphur and lime dissolve in water and when this water comes out in the form of a spring, it contains sulphur. Hence, water of such springs has the smell of sulphur and they are called sulphur springs. In India, there are many such springs in Kashmir, Haryana and Uttar Pradesh.

Sometimes water from the Earth's surface reaches deep down in the Earth's interior. It then starts boiling due to the Earth's heat. When it comes out through such opening in the Earth in the form of a spring, its water is hot. Such springs are called hot springs. There are many such springs in the United States of America and New Zealand. ooo

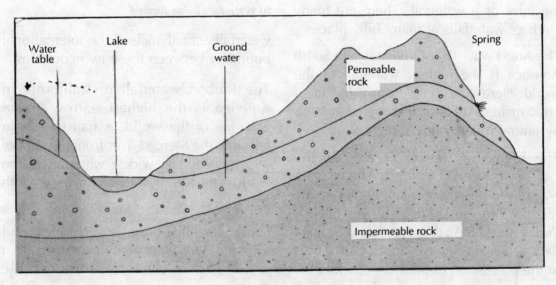

Formation of springs

26

How are waterfalls formed?

A body of water falling down from a mountain rock is known as a waterfall. If water falls from a great height in the form of a large stream, it is called a cataract. But if the falling stream is narrow, it is called a cascade.

It is essential for the formation of a waterfall that water flows through certain hard rocky areas. Hard rocks should be followed by soft soil which water can easily cut through. At some places, due to natural changes, the river flows through areas which are higher than the sea level and thus water falls from a height. Sometimes flow of the river is obstructed by landslides. Water accumulates there and later falls down in the form of a waterfall. There are many kinds of waterfalls at many hilly places.

The Angel waterfall of Venezuela in South America is the highest waterfall of the world. Here water falls from a height of 1000 metres. This was discovered in 1835 by Jimmy Angel, pilot of the US.

The highest waterfall of Asia is the Gersoppa waterfall in India. The Niagara waterfall is also world-famous for many reasons. Situated 25 km Northwest of New York in the U.S.A., this waterfall of Niagara river is divided into two parts. One part is in the possession of the U.S.A., while the other is in possession of Canada. This

a)

b)

a) *Niagara Falls in USA*
b) *Waterfalls being formed*

waterfall actually acts as the international boundary between these two countries.

The Ribbon waterfall of California in America is the highest narrow-stream waterfall of the world. A narrow stream falls into the Merced river from a height of 490 metres. The widest waterfall of the world is the Khoni waterfall having a width of 11 km.

Some waterfalls have proved very useful to man. Hydro-electricity produced from waterfalls is used for innumerable purposes. ○○○

27

What are glaciers ?

Glacier is a large mass of moving ice. We see glaciers in various mountain ranges and vallies of the world. In the Alps alone there are as many as 1,200 glaciers. In the high mountains of the Alaska, there are around thousands of glaciers with length, ranging from 30 to 60 kilometres.

The process for the formation of glaciers is described below. During snowfall snow slides down on the slopes of mountains. After a considerable time it accumulates in big quantities. As this accumulated snow does not melt even in summers, its quantity keeps on increasing. As the quantity of snow increases, the pressure on the lowest layer of the snow also increases. Due to the increased pressure and other atmospheric effects, air leaks out from the lowest layer of snow and consequently, it becomes hardened. This process goes on till a time comes when glaciers become heavy enough to flow downhill under their own weight.

Glaciers are mainly of two kinds. The first type is the **valley glaciers**. When there is snowfall on the mountains, the snow slides down on the slopes. This gets deposited in the spaces between the mountains. When snow accumulates in big quantities, it often starts sliding down. The slow moving river of ice is called the valley glacier. Large chunks of stones coming in the way of this river move forward with this river and break into pieces due to friction and collisions with other stones. They spread uniformly in all directions. The motion of the glacier thus forms valleys.

The second type of glaciers is **continental glaciers**. There are many such glaciers in Greenland. In plains, when the accumulated snow crosses a certain limit, it starts sliding. Such sliding mountains of ice are called the continental glaciers. When these glaciers reach the sea, they break into large chunks of ice and thus icebergs are formed.

Glaciers are found in all the countries of the world. The Zambert glacier of South Australia is the largest glacier of the world. This is 400 km long and 64 km broad. In addition, Zermatt in Switzerland, Lom in Norway, Bosson in France and Nisqually in America are the main glaciers of the world. OOO

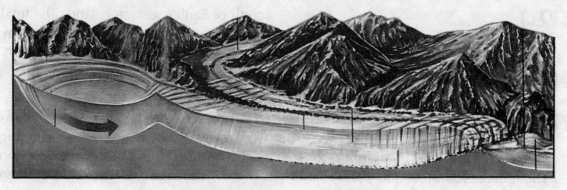

Glaciers carrying rocks and debris with it

143

28

Why is the sea water salty?

Removal of salt from the sea water by evaporation

Everybody knows that sea water is salty. This means that some salt in the dissolved form is present in sea water. One gallon of sea water contains about one hundred grams of salt. In general sea water has 4% to 6% salt in it. In comparison to open seas, the quantity of salt in closed seas like the Mediterranean and the Red Sea is more. If salt of all the oceans is collected and dried, one can make a 288 km high and 1.6 km thick wall with this salt, which will be long enough to encircle the entire perimeter of the Earth along the equator.

Do you know from where this salt comes in the sea water? We know that salt is soluble in water. Rain water carries salt and other minerals present in the Earth's crust to the rivers (which makes river water salty) which, in turn, take them to the ocean. The water of the oceans evaporates to the atmosphere and again falls on to the Earth in the form of rain, but the salt is left in the oceans because salt cannot be evaporated. This cycle has been continuing for millions of years and as a result the salt content of the oceans has been increasing continuously. This explains the presence of large quantities of salt in sea water.

The common salt used every day by us in our kitchens is produced from the sea water or from the water of saline lakes. OOO

29

How were the oceans formed?

About three-fourth of the Earth's total surface is covered with water. Only one-fourth of Earth's surface is land. The total area of the Earth's surface covered by oceans comes to 361.100 million sq. km. Do you know how and when these oceans were formed?

It is not yet fully known when oceans were formed. However, at the beginning of the formation of Earth, there were no oceans. The age of oceans has been calculated on the basis of the minerals present inside them. It is estimated that oceans were formed some time between 500 to 1,000 million years before.

The story of the origin of oceans is very interesting. The Earth was a giant burning fire ball at the time of its birth. Its surface was formed by molten rocks. When the Earth started cooling slowly, it was enveloped by clouds of gases. These clouds became very heavy after cooling. They started raining heavily, but the Earth's surface was still so hot that the raindrops falling on it would evaporate and mix with the atmosphere again. This would again come down to the Earth in the form of rains. This cycle continued for millions of years. The Earth's crust became cold and tough and the rain-water would boil no more, but the heavy down-pour continued for thousands of years. The low-lying areas of the Earth were filled up with the water of these heavy rains. These vast lakes of water on the surface of the Earth are today's oceans. OOO

30

What is Dead Sea ?

Dead Sea is the only sea on earth which has no plant or animal life. It is, therefore, appropriately called Dead Sea. In fact, Dead Sea is a saline lake situated between Jordan and Israel. This is 77 km long and its breadth ranges between 5 to 18 kilometres. The water level of Dead Sea is the lowest on the Earth. It is lower than the sea-level by 396 metres. Millions of years ago the level of Dead Sea was, however, higher than the present one by 427 metres. At that time aquatic animals were living in Dead Sea. All of a sudden, there was a draught and the water of this sea evaporated. Gradually this sea acquired the present state.

No river originates from this sea. The Jordan river and some small canals end up in this sea. Since no river comes out of this, the water of this sea depletes only by evaporation. Consequently, the amount of salt and other soluble minerals brought into the sea by the Jordan river and other smaller canals goes on increasing. You will be surprised to know that the amount of salt present in Dead Sea is the largest in comparison to the other seas. In general, the amount of salt present in any sea is 4% to 6%. But even this make you sick as it contains large quantities of magnesium chloride and other poisonous substances. Due to the presence of large quantities of salt and other poisonous materials no living being can survive in this sea. Hence fish and other acquatic animals of the Jordan river die as soon as they enter the water of this sea. OOO

31

Are there mountains inside the sea ?

Generally, sea mountains are those mountains which are at least one kilometre above the seabed. A number of such mountains have been discovered.

Upheavals at the bottom of the sea are responsible for the formation of these mountains. Volcanic eruptions in the seabed also make mountains. Generally, these mountains are one to three kilometres high. Majority of these mountains remain submerged in water, but some of them have surfaced above also. The flat mountains coming above water are called islands. The Hawaii islands were formed in this manner.

There are many mountains in the midst of oceans. The mid-ocean ridge is continuous and it winds for 60,000 km through all the world's oceans. There are many mountains in the north-east part of the Pacific Ocean. Most of these mountains are submerged in water, but some of the mountains of the Hawaiian chain have surfaced above. They are called the Hawaii Islands. The highest mountain of the Hawaiian chain is the Mauna Kea. The height of this mountain is 4,200 metres above sea level, but the total height of this mountain from the bottom of the sea is 9,686 metres. That means the height of this mountain inside the sea is 5,486 metres. If its height is taken in full, this is the highest mountain of the world. ○○○

The flat mountains above water form island

146

6
The Universe

- How did the universe come into existence? • What is the Milky Way? • How are stars formed? • Why are some stars brighter than others? • What is the Solar System? • What is the Sun? • What are the Sun spots? • What is Solar Eclipse? • What are Meteorites? • What is the Moon's force of gravity? • What are Comets? • What are the rings of the Saturn? • What is Moon—the only satellite of the Earth? • How distant are stars from us? • What is lunar eclipse? • What is the Zodiac? • Is there life on other planets?

1

How did the universe come into existence?

The universe includes the Sun, Earth, solar system, galaxies and everything else that exitsts. Even with the most powerful telescopes, astronomers can not see the limit of the universe. Most scientists believe, however, the universe is mostly a vast empty space.

Now the question that arises is how did this universe come into existence? There are many theories regarding its origin. According to one theory, the entire matter in the beginning of the universe was like a fire-ball. At a certain time, a big explosion took place and the matter of this giant fire ball got scattered in all directions. On cooling down these scattered parts gave birth to the galaxies. The matter of these galaxies has been expanding continuously.

This incident took place around 20 billion years ago. Obviously, if this expansion continues, it will make the universe empty.

However, according to another theory, because of the force of gravitation, a time will come when the expansion of the galaxies will stop, and they will start contracting. This suggests a pulsating universe. Again, according to a third theory, new galaxies are constantly under formation and the matter of the older galaxies goes on scattering. This is the theory of the balanced universe. It is difficult to say which of the three theories is authentic. However, in order to propound a correct theory regarding the origin of the universe and its existence, researches are still in process. OOO

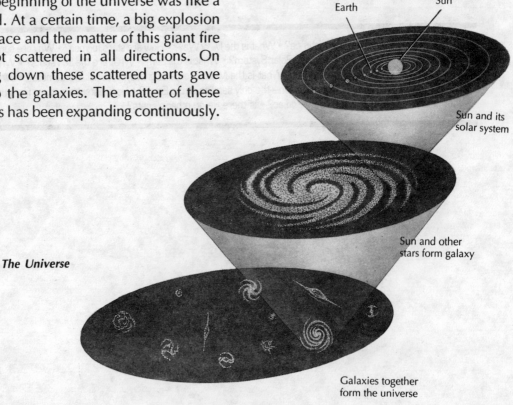

Earth   Sun

Sun and its solar system

Sun and other stars form galaxy

The Universe

Galaxies together form the universe

2

What is the Milky Way?

When we look at the sky in the night, a dim strip of milky colour extending far and wide is seen. This is our Milky Way or 'Akash Ganga'. With the help of the powerful telescopes, it has been observed that the Milky Way contains innumerable stars, dust and gases. Its milky colour is due to the presence of cluster of stars. The Solar System also belongs to this galaxy. There are billions of such galaxies in the universe.

Scientists have studied the shape, size and structure of the Milky Way with the help of the powerful telescopes. It is like a lens, whose central part is very thick and edges are thin. Our Solar System is situated at the thin edge. When we look at the sky, we are, in fact, looking at the centre of the Milky Way. That is why the stars present in it seem to have clustered together. Studies have revealed that the Milky Way is spiral-shaped. It has around 150 trillion stars.

Do you know the size of the Milky Way? Its size can not be measured in terms of kilometres. There is a separate unit for measuring large distances. This unit is called a light year, which is the distance travelled by light in a year. We know that light travels with a velocity of 30 thousand (3×10^5) km per second. In a year, it will travel a distance of 9 million million km. This distance is called one light year. The diameter of Milky Way is one hundred thousand light years. The sun is located at a distance of 30 thousand light years from the centre of the Milky Way. Our sun also revolves around this Milky Way and takes 225 million years to complete one revolution.

If we look carefully at the Milky Way, some black parts are also seen. These are the regions which have less stars and more dust. ○○○

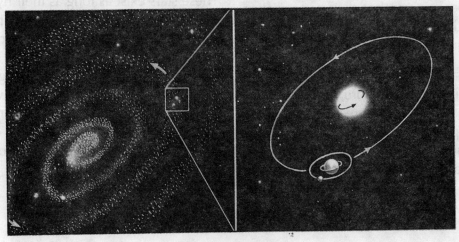

The Milky Way

3

How are stars formed?

We see innumerable stars in the sky every night. Some of the stars are very bright while others are dim. Some are small, others are big. You must be curious to know how stars came into existence.

All these stars, in fact, have evolved from the gases and clouds of particles spread in space. Whenever such clouds or gases due to their own gravitational pull, contract, they get transformed into a spherical ball. In order to evaluate it to convert into a star, the weight of such a cloud should be thousand times more than that of the sun. When such a cloud starts contracting, the pressure so generated produces heat. A portion of this heat is radiated out in various directions. This helps the cloud to further contract. A stage is reached when the cloud is broken into several pieces and every piece goes on contracting. When these pieces become very hot, they start radiating light and then each shining piece becomes a self-luminous star.

These stars continue their contraction further till the temperature, at their centres reaches millions of degree centigrade. At this temperature thermo-nuclear reactions start. These reactions are similar to those which take place in a hydrogen bomb. In

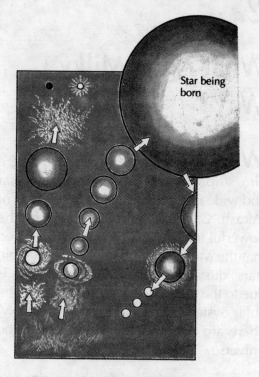

Evolution of Stars

these reactions four nucleus of hydrogen combine to form a helium nucleus. The emission of energy from the stars is caused by these reactions.

These stars exist as long as their hydrogen content does not go below ten percent. Their life span extends to billions of years. Our Sun is also a star in which thermonuclear reactions are going on. As a result of these reactions, we have been receiving heat and light energy from the Sun constantly. It is estimated that our Sun will live for 10 billion years. Half of its life is, of course, over. ооо

4

Why are some stars brighter than others?

If you look at the sky in the night you will observe that some stars are brighter than others. On viewing through powerful telescopes, we not only observe a difference in their brightness, but also in their colours.

The brightness and colour of the stars, in fact, depend on their temperature. The higher the temperature, the brighter is the star.

The relationship between colour and temperature helps in determining the brightness of a star. The Stars whose colour appears to be red or orange are colder than those whose colour is yellow or green. 'White' stars are hotter than 'yellow' or 'green' stars, and that the 'blue' stars have the highest surface temperature.

The surface temperature of 'blue' stars is around 27,750° C or even more. The Sun is a 'yellow' star and as such its temperature is much less than that of the 'blue' stars. Its surface temperature is nearly 6,000° C. The stars which appear to be red are colder and less bright. Their surface temperature is around 1,650° C or even less. All these facts make it clear that the brightness of stars is related to their surface temperature. Since brightness is reduced by distance, stars with very high surface temperature but at a great distance from us, look less bright than those whose surface temperature is less but are nearer to the Earth.   OOO

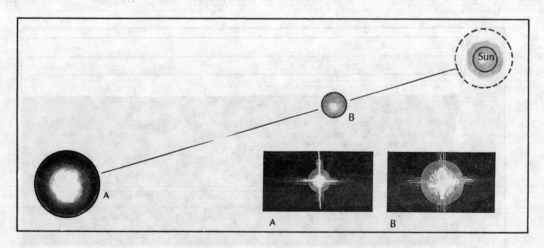

Stars A and B as seen from Earth. B is seen brighter from Earth, but in real is smaller and fainter than A.

5

What is the Solar System?

The Solar System consists of the Sun, the nine planets and their moons, asteriods comets, meteoroids and other debris. The Sun holds all these objects in fixed orbits by its strong gravitational pull. The Sun makes up 99% of the solar system's mass. Most of the solar system is a vast emply space.

The study of the nine planets is necessary for the study of the Solar System.

Mercury: Mercury is the smallest planet of the Solar System and nearest to the Sun. It takes 88 days to complete one revolution round the Sun and the same time to complete one rotation on its own axis. It is difficult to see it very clearly because of its extreme proximity to the Sun. However, studies reveal that there are many hills on its surface. There is no water on this planet. Its distance from the Sun is 58 million kms or 36 million miles.

Venus: Venus is the planet nearest to the Earth. Its distance from the Sun is 108 million km. It is approximately of the same size and weight as is the earth. It takes 224.7 days to complete one revolution round the Sun and thirty days to complete one rotation on its own axis. It has some atmosphere. Man has already launched his spacecraft on this planet.

Earth: Earth is the only planet of the Solar System that is inhabited by living beings. Its distance from the Sun is 150 million km. It takes $365\frac{1}{4}$ days to complete one revolution round the Sun. To complete

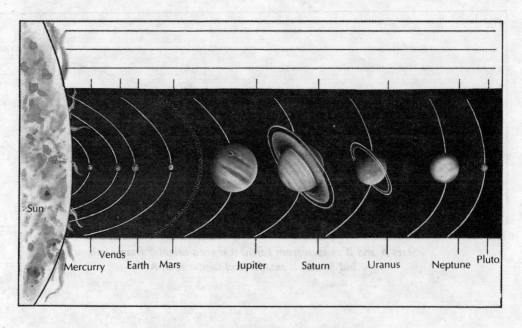

Sun
Mercurry Venus Earth Mars Jupiter Saturn Uranus Neptune Pluto

The Solar System showing planets in order

one rotation on its own axis, it takes about 24 hours. The Moon is a satellite of the Earth and revolves round it.

Mars: Mars is red in appearance. Besides the Earth, this is the only planet where signs of vegetation are found. Studies have revealed that it has mounts of ice on its poles. Its distance from the Sun is 228 million km. It takes about 687 days to make one revolution round the Sun. On its own axis, it makes one rotation in 24 hours and 37 minutes. It has two small moons—Phogos and Diamos.

Jupiter: Jupiter is the biggest planet of the solar family. Its distance from the Sun is 778 million km. or 484 million miles. It completes one revolution round the Sun in 11.8 years, whereas it makes one rotation on its own axis in 9 hours and 50 minutes. It is 317 times heavier than the Earth. Being at a great distance from the Sun, it is an extremely cold planet. It has altogether 14 moons.

Saturn: Saturn is a peculiar planet of the Solar System. Its distance from the Sun is 1,427 million km. It takes $29\frac{1}{2}$ years to complete one revolution round the Sun, but only 10 hours and 14 minutes to make one rotation on its own axis. There are many rings round it. It has 10 moons.

Uranus: Uranus completes one revolution round the Sun in 84 years. But it takes 10 hours and 49 minutes to make one rotation on its own axis. Its distance from the Sun is 2,870 km. It has five moons.

Neptune: Neptune takes 164.8 years in making one revolution round the Sun. It completes one rotation on its own axis in about 15 hours and 48 minutes. Its distance from the Sun is 4,497 million km. It has two moons.

Pluto: Pluto is the farthest planet from the Sun. It completes one revolution of the Sun in 248.4 years. On its own axis it takes 153 hours to complete one rotation. Its distance from the Sun is 5,900 million km. It has one moon.

In addition to these planets, there are about 1,700 asteroids which also revolve round the Sun. They lie between Mars and Jupiter. They are, in fact, small pieces broken away from the bigger planets and since have been revolving round the Sun.

OOO

6

What is the Sun?

Sun is one of the billions of stars in the sky. It forms the nucleus of the Solar System. All planets revolve around the Sun in elliptical orbits. It looks bright and big because of its nearness to the Earth than the other stars. It is at a distance of 150 million kilometres from the earth. Its diameter is 13,92,000 km, compared to the Earth's diameter of 12,756 km. Its volume is approximately 1.3 million times more than that of the Earth. Even though it is gaseous, it weighs more than 300,000 times as much as the earth. It takes 8 minutes 20 seconds for its rays to reach the Earth.

Like other heavenly bodies, the Sun also is not static. It, along with its family of nine planets, revolves round the Milky Way and takes about 225 million years to complete one revolution. It also rotates on its own axis. The temperature at its centre is approximately 15 million degree centigrade. The solar surface is composed of three gaseous layers. The inner most layer is called 'photosphere'. Its temperature is 6000° C. The solar spots are seen on this very layer. The next layer is 'chromosphere' which is approximately 14,000 km thick. This is composed of hydrogen, helium and other gases. The temperature of this layer is about 5000° C. The outer layer of the Sun is called 'corona'.

The Sun not only gives light to the Earth, but also gives life to its inhabitants. The Sun is the biggest source of heat and energy. Without it, there is, of course, no question of life on the Earth.   ○○○

The Sun

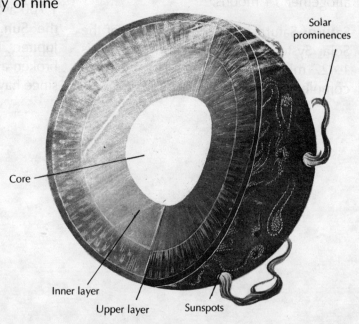

Solar prominences

Core

Inner layer

Upper layer   Sunspots

7

What are the Sun spots?

The most spectacular feature of the Sun's surface is the 'Sunspots'. Galileo was the first man to observe these spots in 1610 with the help of his telescope. Through the telescope the Sunspots looked like dark holes on the shining surface of the Sun.

These spots often appear in groups. They increase in number, then diminish in regular cycles. These cycles repeat every seventh, eleventh or fourteenth year. The portion of the Sun having these spots, emits light of less intensity. According to modern scientific theories, these spots are formed by reactions between the electrically charged gases of the Sun and solar magnetic fields. When at any place on the Sun, strong magnetic field develops, the temperature of that place is lowered. Consequently, these portions appear as black spots amidst hotter and brighter portions. The temperature of these spots is approximately 4000° C. They are not permanent but go on changing.

Can you imagine the size of these spots? Some spots are big enough to accommodate hundreds of earths. Even a small spot is so big that it can cover two-

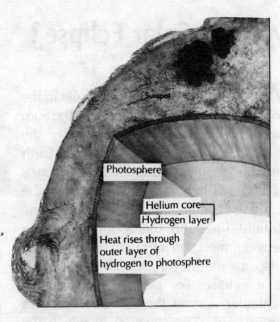

Sun Spots

thousandth part of the Sun's surface. These spots are spread over an area of 500 million square miles on the Sun. On June 4, 1946 scientists saw a Sunspot measuring 4,80,000 km in length and 1,12,000 km in breadth. Most of the solar spots last for a few days only. But some may last for two months or even more.

It is inferred from the change of state of Sunspots that, like the earth, the Sun is also rotating on its own axis. These spots are moving from East to West because the Sun is moving from East to West. Changes occur in the location, sizes and rotation period of these spots. ○○○

8

What is Solar Eclipse?

We know that the Earth is a planet in the Solar System and revolves around the Sun. Similarly the Moon is a satellite of the Earth and revolves around it. The Earth and the Moon cast long shadows in space as the Sun's light falls on them. When the Sun, the Earth and the Moon come in one straight line and the Moon comes in between the Earth and the Sun, the Moon obscures the Sun from our view. This is solar eclipse. For people living in that particular part of the earth, it becomes almost dark. The situation in which the Sun, the Moon and the Earth come in a straight line occurs only on new moon-days. The solar eclipse, therefore, takes place only on new moon-days.

However, the solar eclipse does not take place on every new moon-day. The reason for this is that the plane of earth's orbit makes an angle of 5° with the orbit plane of the Moon. Had their orbits been in the same plane, we would have seen solar eclipse on every new moon day. Because of this angle, the revolving moon is sometimes above and sometimes below the orbit plane of the Earth. Only sometimes they come in one straight line.

By knowing the position of the Earth, the Sun and the Moon, solar eclipse and its duration, can be predicted in advance. If the Moon obstructs the full Sun, there is total solar eclipse and if the Moon obstructs only a part of the Sun, it will be a partial solar eclipse. In total solar eclipse, the edge of the Sun is visible.

Total solar eclipses are of great importance to the scientists as, during the period of eclipse, the shining edge of the Sun and other parts can be easily studied. Solar eclipse can take place twice a year or five times at the most. During 1935 there were five solar eclipses. In 1982 four solar eclipses took place. The total solar eclipse which took place on February 16, 1980 and was seen in India, lasted for a very long time. OOO

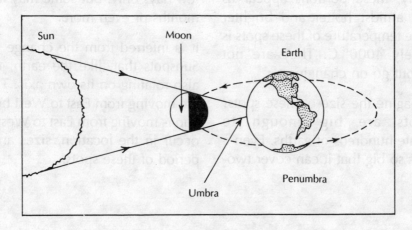

Solar Eclipse

156

9

What are Meteorites?

When we look at the sky during the night, we sometime see a star falling and making a streak of light in the atmosphere as it falls. Ultimately, it disappears. It, in fact, disintegrates. Such heavenly bodies falling after disintegration are not stars—they are meteorites. They are of varying sizes.

Whenever any one of the celestial bodies, while making revolutions, comes nearer to the earth, it is attracted towards the earth due to its force of gravitation. Attraction of the earth increases the velocity of the body and this, in turn, increases friction with the atmospheric air. Consequently, it becomes very hot. As a result of this, hot gases start coming out of it. These gases start burning and the atmosphere is lighted. The sound of friction in the air is heard over long distance. Because of heat and friction, the body disintegrates into small pieces which are scattered in the atmosphere. But some of these meteorites are so big that they are not completely destroyed in the atmosphere and some of their parts fall on the earth.

Meteorites become visible to us only when they are in the atmosphere, at a height of 112 km from the earth. Majority of them are destroyed in the atmosphere by the time they come down to a height of 80 km. Their downward velocity ranges from 160 km to 200 km per sec. They fall down both during the day and the night, but they are not visible during the day because of the bright sunlight.

Meteorites are, in fact, pieces of comets. Whenever the earth approaches the orbit of some comet, some pieces of it are attracted towards the earth. These pieces may be either big or small. The biggest meteorite reaching the earth weighed 37 tons.

There are three kinds of meteorites. The first kind is called the shooting star. A

Falling Meteorites

meteor of this kind is like a dim-lighted star. The second is a meteoric stone. It is so big that some part of it reaches the earth. The third kind is the fire ball. Even if it is big, it is destroyed in the atmosphere itself. The outer layer of the meteorites is hot, but their inner layers are cold. Because of the melting of the outer layer, a thin shining layer gets deposited outside. In many meteorites, there are craters like the ones caused on human faces by small-pox. The formation of meteorites is similar to that of ordinary crystalline stones on the Earth. Their crystalline nature suggests that

they must have been in molten state at some stage. Quite often the meteorites are composed of stones, iron, nickel and other elements.

The Arizona Meteor Crater measures 1,265 m across and it is 175 m deep. This crater was formed about 25,000 years ago by a meteorite fall.

In India, some meteoric stones are preserved in the museum of Calcutta. However, bigger stones have not been collected. In the US, samples of 672 meteorites have been kept in various museums.   ooo

10

What is the Moon's force of gravity?

All bodies of the universe attract each other. This force of attraction is called the force of gravitation. It was Newton who propounded the law of gravitation. The force of gravitation between two bodies depends upon two things — their masses and the distance between them. The greater the masses of the bodies, the greater will be the force of attraction. But, with the increase distance between them, the force as a consequence decreases. As a matter of fact, if the distance between two bodies is doubled, the force of attraction will be reduced to one-fourth.

The Moon is a satellite of the Earth. It revolves round the Earth. The mass of the Earth is about 81 times more than that of the Moon while the Moon is only a quarter of the Earth's diameter. The gravitational pull of the Moon is only one-sixth of the Earth's gravity. If a man can jump one metre high on the Earth, he can jump six metres high on the Moon. Similarly, if a ball is thrown up from the surface of the Moon, it will go up six times higher than it would on the Earth.

The Moon does not have atmosphere because of its low force of gravity. As a result, air molecules cannot be attracted towards it and they fail to stay around it. The Moon's gravitational pull affects our Earth also. Because of this pull, water in the seas is attracted upwards causing tides.   ooo

11

What are Comets?

The shining celestial bodies with tails are called comets. They are the members of the solar system and also revolve round the sun in definite orbits. Every comet has two parts—head and tail. They are very big in size. Many of them are so big that their heads alone are many times bigger than the sun. Their tails are millions of miles long.

Comets are made up of rocks, dust and gases. Their tails contain ammonia, methane, water vapour and ice particles. As the sun-light falls on them, they shine. Some comets are very bright and can be seen with naked eyes but others can be observed only with the help of telescopes. Scientists have been constantly studying these comets with the help of telescopes. It is estimated that on an average, nine new comets are discovered every year.

Halley's comet is the biggest amongst the comets discovered so far. It comes near the earth after every 75½ years and only then it becomes visible. This was seen for the first time by the famous astronomer Edmund Halley of England in 1682, and was named after him. This was subsequently observed in 1758, 1835 and 1910. Between September 1909 and July 1911, many studies were conducted about this comet with the help of powerful telescopes. It was last seen in 1986 when space probe Giotto took its close-up photographs. It is estimated that this will be again visible in the year 2061. Some comets come near the earth after few years, but there are others which take thousands of years in this process, as they take thousands of years to complete one revolution around the sun. Sometimes the comets approaching the earth are crushed to dust and then meteoric dust falls on the earth.

It is now believed that comets are born out of the dust generated by the bursting of volcanoes from some planets or satellites. Some scientists contend that they were formed simultaneously with the solar system. But, till now the scientists are not certain about their origin.   ∞

Halley's Comet

159

12

What are the rings of the Saturn?

Saturn with its rings

Saturn is the second largest planet of the Solar System. On the basis of the distance from the Sun, this is the sixth planet. Its distance from the Sun is 1,427 million km. Its intense brightness is due to its bigger size. It keeps on revolving round the Sun and takes about 291½ years to complete one revolution. It has seventeen moons revolving round it. It appears yellow in colour. It is 96 times heavier than the Earth, while its volume is 743.7 times more than that of the Earth.

Saturn is the most peculiar of all the planets. Its peculiarity lies in the rings surrounding it. These rings are not visible to the naked eyes but can be seen very clearly with the help of telescopes. In July, 1610 when Galileo studied it with the help of his telescope, he saw some unknown materials stuck to this planet on all sides. In 1655, a scientist named Christian Huygen discovered with the help of a powerful telescope that Saturn is surrounded by a ring which does not touch its main body at any point.

With the help of powerful telescopes, three rings are seen very clearly. In 1969 scientists discovered a fourth ring also. The four rings of Saturn are called A, B, C, and D rings. The total width of these rings is about 274,000 km. which is twice the diameter of Saturn. Scientists are of the view that these rings might have been formed by minute particles of dust and ice.

The outermost ring A which is somewhat brighter has its outer diameter to be 274,000 km. and its inner diameter to be 2,38,400 km. Its width is about 16,000 km. The distance between A and B rings is 4,000 km. The B ring is the brightest. Its outer diameter is 2,30,400 km, and the inner diameter is 1,79,200 km. Its outer part is brighter than inner part. Its width is about 25,600 km. The distance between B and C rings is about 960 km. The C ring is not bright. Its outer diameter is 1,77,600 km and whereas the inner diameter is 1,43,920 km. The fourth is the D ring. This is very dim and hence it is difficult to locate its boundaries.

All these rings appear elliptical. From the earth, all these rings appear to be connected with each other. Of all the planets Saturn is the only planet which has such rings. OOO

13

What is Moon—the only satellite of the Earth?

The Moon is a heavenly body. Any heavenly body that revolves round a planet is called its satellite. The Moon revolves round the Earth. Therefore, it is called a satellite of the Earth.

The Moon is the only satellite on which man has landed. On July 20, 1969, Neil Armstrong, an American astronaut, succeeded for the first time in landing on the Moon's surface in Apollo 11 flight and unravelled many mysteries about it. In this very flight, a retro-reflector was mounted on the Moon's surface. Laser beams sent from the Earth's surface and reflected back by this retro-reflector enabled scientists to calculate the exact distance of the Moon from the Earth. The distance so calculated has an accuracy of less than 15 cm. The distance has been calculated to be 3,84,400 km.

The Moon is a solid spherical body like a football. It completes one revolution round the Earth in an elliptical path in a period of 29 days 12 hours and 43 minutes. We call this period a lunar month. Only one side of the Moon is always visible to us because the period of its rotation on its axis is approximately the same as the period of its revolution round the Earth.

The Moon

The Moon does not have its own light but shines due to the Sun-light. Ten percent of the Sun's light falling on the Moon is reflected by its surface while the rest is absorbed by it. During noon, the surface temperature of the Moon is about 130°C, while, during the night, it is very cold. The Moon's surface is very uneven. There are mountains, valleys and black plains on the Moon's surface. These black portions appear as lunar spots. There are heaps of ash on its surface caused by the fall of meteors. The diameter of the largest crater on the Moon is 232 km which is 365.7 metres deep. Studies on the samples of rocks collected from the Moon's surface have revealed that they contain metals like aluminium, iron, magnesium etc. The lunar surface contains silicates also. The Moon does not have air and water and, therefore, there are no signs of life there.

The average distance of the Moon from

the Earth keeps on changing slightly because of the Moon's elliptical orbit. The diameter of the Moon is approximately 3476 km. It rotates on its axis with a speed of 3430 km per hour. The Earth is about 81.3 times heavier than the Moon and 49 times larger in volume. The force of gravity on the Moon is one-sixth that of the Earth. Scientists are making constant efforts to obtain more and more information about the Moon.

OOO

14

How distant are stars from us ?

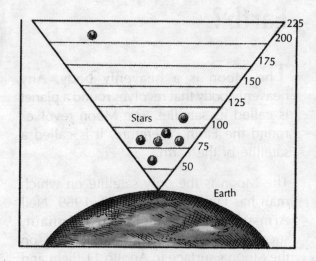

Distance of the stars forming the plough constellation from Earth

Billions of stars which we see in the sky every night are made up of hot gases. Even the Sun is a star. However, there are stars which are million times more shining than the Sun, but they don't appear so because of their greater distances from the earth. The stars are of varying sizes.

We measure the distance of stars in units of light years. A light year is the distance travelled by light (its velocity being 3×10^5 km or 3 hundred thousand km per second) in one year. The star nearest to the earth (other than the Sun) is Proxima Centauri. Its distance from the earth is 4.28 light years. This star is visible only in the Southern Hemisphere. The nearest star visible in the Northern Hemisphere is Sirius. Its distance from the earth is 8.8 light years. In addition to this, another neighbouring star is Alpha Centauri which is 4.37 light years away from us.

The farthest star from the earth which is visible with our naked eye is more than eight million light years away from us. If we use powerful telescopes, we can even see stars that are 1000 times more distant than this one. Some stars are so far away from the earth that light from them takes more than 1,000 million years to reach the earth.

Scientists have developed various kinds of optical and radio telescopes to study stars. They have gained considerable knowledge relating to the heavenly bodies with the help of these telescopes. OOO

Plough as seen from the Earth

15

What is lunar eclipse?

When we stand in the sunlight, the rays of the Sun fall on us and we can see our shadows. Exactly like this, shadows of the Earth and the Moon are also formed in the space due to the Sun rays falling on them. Since the Earth and the Moon are spherical in shape, their shadows are conical in shape. These shadows are very long. The larger the distance of a body from the Sun, the longer will be its shadow. Lunar eclipse is darkness on the Moon due to the Earth's shadow over a portion of it.

While making their revolutions, the Sun, the Earth, and the Moon come in a straight line and the Earth sometimes comes in between the Sun and the Moon, thus the shadow of the Earth falls on the Moon. In other words, the Sunlight does not fall on the Moon when the Earth comes in between the two. The portion over which the shadow falls becomes dark. This is called lunar eclipse. Such a situation occurs only on Purnima (full Moon) days. Therefore, the lunar eclipse takes place only on that day. If the Earth's shadow covers the entire Moon, it is total lunar eclipse. If the shadow covers only a part of the Moon, it is partial eclipse. Generally, there are three lunar eclipses in a year, out of which one is a total lunar eclipse.

Now the question arises: when the full Moon comes every month, why does lunar eclipse not take place every month? The reason is that the plane of the Moon's orbit makes an angle of 5° with the plane of the Earth's orbit. Consequently, the Moon revolves either above or below the Earth's shadow. So, it is only twice or thrice a year that all the three—the Sun, the Moon, and the Earth—come in one straight line. Hence the lunar eclipse does not take place every month. Astronomers, using mathematical calculations, easily predict the time and duration of the lunar eclipse. ○○○

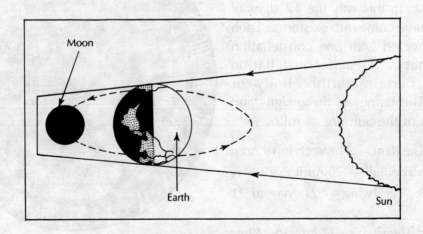

Position of Sun and Moon during Lunar Eclipse

163

16

What is the Zodiac?

In ancient times, when people looked up at the sky in the night, they observed many bright stars arranged in a certain pattern or group. Each group is called a constellation. It means a group of stars. Studies of movements of these constellations led to the discovery that they move in space in fixed directions. The number of constellations visible during the year at different times was found to be 12. The Sun and the Moon were always seen rising and setting in the same directions in which these twelve constellations were located. These 12 constellations were called the signs of the zodiac.

The hypothetical part of the sky through which the Sun, the Moon and other planets seem to be passing is called the zodiac. Each of the 12 constellations situated at an angle of 30°, is named as a different sign of the zodiac. In this way the 12 signs of the zodiac have come into existence. Each sign is connected with one constellation and the shape of each constellation resembles certain earthly body or substance. The names of these signs and the position of the Sun are as follows:

(i) **Aries:** The Ram — 21 March to 19 April

(ii) **Taurus:** The Bull — 20 April to 20 May

(iii) **Gemini:** The Twins — 21 May to 21 June

(iv) **Cancer:** The Crab — 22 June to 22 July

(v) **Leo:** The Lion — 23 July to 22 August

(vi) **Virgo:** The Virgin — 23 August to 22 September

(vii) **Libra:** The Balance — 23 September to 23 October

(viii) **Scorpio:** The Scorpion — 24 October to 21 November

(ix) **Sagittarius:** The Archer — 22 November to 21 December

(x) **Capricorn:** The Goat — 22 December to 19 January

(xi) **Aquarius:** The Water Bearer — 20 January to 18 February

(xii) **Pisces:** The Fish — 19 February to 20 March

In other words, these are the 12 constellations through which the Sun appears passing during a year e.g. during 21 March to 19 April, the Sun is supposed to pass through the constellation Aries or Ram; during 20 April to 20 May, through Taurus and so on till it reaches Pisces.

The science of astrology is based on these

A calendar to study zodiac signs

12 signs of the zodiac. Astrologers use the dates given above. In addition to these twelve constellations, in the ancient times, people knew of 36 more constellations. Thus, during olden times, people had knowledge of 48 constellations.

Subsequently, astronomers discovered 40 other constellations. Thus, man knows about 88 constellations. The Hydra constellation is the biggest amongst them. This has at least 78 such stars that can be seen without any aid.　　　OOO

17

Is there life on other planets ?

The question whether there is life on planets other than the Earth has often perplexed scientists. If it is true that there is life on planets other than the Earth, what could be the possible ways of establishing contact with the living beings of other planets?

It is felt that only radio can help to solve this problem. In 1960 American scientists received radio signals from some stars that created a hope about the existence of life on some other heavenly bodies. However, they could not get any concrete evidence to prove this.

A few years ago, people talked of having

seen some unidentified flying objects (UFO'S) in the sky at many places. It was observed that the flying objects were shaped like saucers. People called them flying saucers. This led scientists to think of the possibility of life on other planets as well. It was felt that these saucers were extra-terrestrial attempts at scientific experiments. These saucers had different shapes. Some of them were round while others were cigar shaped. Many stories were heard about their colours. Their speed was reported to be very high.

These flying saucers have also been photographed. They were even chased by aeroplanes. A thorough study of these objects revealed that the so-called flying saucers were either balloons launched for weather studies or some meteoric bodies. Now scientists are of the view that the Earth is the only planet which has favourable conditions for the existence of life. Scientists have not found any other planet in the universe where there is life.　　　OOO

7
Scientists & Inventions

• Who invented transistor? • How was the telephone invented? • What is Superconductivity? • How was the submarine invented? • How was the rocket developed? • What is an Atom Bomb? • What is a radar and how does it work? • How does an Aerosol spray work? • How does an Electric Typewriter work? • How does a Zip Fastener work?

1

Who invented transistor ?

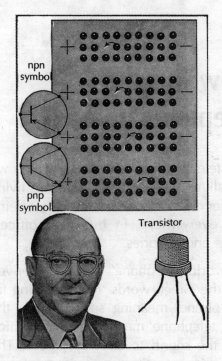

John Bardeen

A transistor is a tiny solid state device used to control and amplify an electric signal. Transistors are now used in place of vacuum tubes in many electronic circuits. Transistors are smaller, weigh less, last longer and are less expensive than vacuum tubes. They consume less electricity and produce less heat than vacuum tubes.

Transistor was first developed in 1948 by three American Physicists, John Bardeen, William Shockley and Walter Brattain. These three won the Nobel Prize for physics in 1956. The development of transistor revolutionized the world of electronics.

A transistor is made of a semiconductor such as silicon or germanium with certain amount of impurities doped in them. When impurities of V A group like arsenic or phosphorus are doped in the semiconductor material, it becomes a n-type semiconductor (n-for the negatively-charged electrons). On the other hand, if III A group elements like Aluminium are doped, it becomes a p-type semiconductor (p-for positively-charged holes).

Transistors are of two types-junction and field effect. Junction transistors are again of two types *npn* and *pnp*. In an *npn* transistor, the middle layer is p-type while the two outer layers are both n-type. The middle layer is the base, one outside layer is the emitter and the other outside layer is the collector.

Another type of junction transistor is *pnp* transistor which contains a layer of n-type semiconductor sandwitched between two layers of p-type semiconductor. In the *pnp* transistor, the positively charged holes move from emitter to collector.

In a field effect transistor, there are only two layers of semiconductor. The current flowing through one of the layers, the channel, is controlled by a voltage connected to the other layer, the gate.

Transistors are used in computers, stereos, radios, televisions, satellites and many other electronic circuits. OOO

2

How was the telephone invented?

The telephone is a device by which we can talk to our friends and relatives living in other cities or countries even. It is being used everywhere, in business, offices, homes and factories.

The world 'telephone' has been derived from the Greek words 'tele' meaning far and 'phone' meaning sound. Thus, the word 'telephone' means the device which takes the sound to faraway places. The story of its invention is very interesting. It goes back to June 2, 1875, when Alexander Graham Bell was working alongwith his assistant Thomas Watson on some problem related to telegraphy. Bell was on the telegraphic receiver in one room, whereas

his assistant was in another room. Watson created some vibrations on an iron strip. Bell rushed to the other room and found that the iron strip vibrating between the poles of a magnet was producing electric current in the connecting wire. It was this historic observation which led to the birth of telephone. He was able to demonstrate the telephonic conversation on March 10, 1876.

Do you know how the telephone works? It has two main parts: the mouthpiece and the earpiece. The mouthpiece of the telephone works as a transmitter whereas the earpiece works as a receiver. Both are enclosed in one cage and are connected by the line wire. When we speak into the mouthpiece, a diaphragm attached to it starts vibrating. And in accordance to these vibrations a varying current is produced. This current is carried by the telephone line wire to the receiver of another telephone. This varying current produces vibrations in the diaphragm attached to

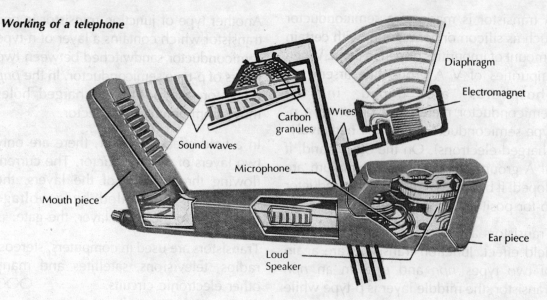

Working of a telephone

Mouth piece

Sound waves

Carbon granules

Wires

Microphone

Loud Speaker

Diaphragm

Electromagnet

Ear piece

the receiver which is then converted into original sound waves. The person at the other end hears clearly the voice of the speaker. The same process is repeated between our receiver and the mouthpiece of the telephone at the other end. In this way two persons can talk to each other on the telephone.

Today, every country has a vast network of telephone lines. Thus world has become very small. Thanks to the telephones!

OOO

3

What is Superconductivity ?

In 1911, Heike Kamerlingh Onnes, a Dutch Physicist, invented the phenomenon of superconductivity. He observed that at liquid helium temperature (4.2K) the resistance of mercury totally disappeared. He called this dramatic decrease in resistance as the phenomenon of superconductivity. It was also observed that near absolute zero, several other metals suddenly show near zero electrical resistance. For this outstanding discovery Kemerlingh Onnes was awarded the Nobel prize of Physics in 1913.

The theory of superconductivity was devised in 1957 by J. Bardeen, L.N. Cooper and J.R. Schrieffer. This is known as BCS theory.

For the last 45 years, scientists all over the world are busy in searching superconducting materials for room temperature use. Niobium-tin alloy is one material which shows superconduction at 18K. Niobium-germanium is a superconductor at 23K. In 1986, L.X. Mueller developed lanthanum-barium which is superconductor at 35K. In 1987, Ching Wu Chu developed Yttrium barium and copper with a transition temperature of 94K. In India many research laboratories such as NPL, TIFR, Saha Institute of Nuclear Physics etc. are carrying out research in the field of superconductivity.

Superconductivity may bring new revolutions in many fields. Superconductors may make overhead electrical transmission more efficient and less costly. The power requirements of electric motors and electromagnets would become minimal with the windings of superconducting wires. Traditional wheel may be replaced by magnetic levitation. New superconductive switches and memory cells for computers are being developed using the phenomenon of superconductivity. OOO

4

How was the submarine invented?

The submarine is a vessel which is closed from all sides and is capable of easily floating both on the surface of water and under water. It can go very deep into the sea.

Since long, man has made efforts to reach the bottom of the seas in search of diamonds and pearls. In order to succeed in his attempts he tried to invent some device which could go under water. Thus, first submarine — the boat capable of travelling under water — was devised by Carnelius Van Drebbele of Holland in 1620. This submarine was made up of wood and was wrapped in leather. This could go up to the depth of 3 to 4 metres into the sea water. Thereafter, efforts were made to develop other types of submarines. Up to the end of eighteenth century, various types of submarines were made. Till 1727, fourteen different types of submarines had been made in England alone.

In 1880, a submarine propelled by the steam engine was developed. Later on submarines powered by gasoline and electricity came into operation. Submarines were successfully used in First World War (1914-18). And during the Second World War (1939-45), submarines powered by diesel were also used in sea warfare. Now

A submarine

even nuclear powered submarines have been developed. Modern submarines are made from steel sheets. They are equipped with instruments like periscopes, sonars and radars. The periscopes enable seamen to keep an eye on the situation at the water's surface. Sonars help in locating the other submarines and torpedoes. There are also arrangements in submarines for breathing. Nuclear submarines have no problem of smoke and gas generated by fuels.

These days submarines are being used for various purposes. They are very useful in oceanography. Missiles and torpedoes are launched from them to destroy the enemy ships. Modern submarines can also attack and destroy the enemy's submarines. Every submarine has arrangements that help its crew to escape to safety in case of danger.

OOO

5

How was the rocket developed?

Today, the word 'rocket' is used in many forms. Missiles used in wars are also a form of rockets. The space-ships used to collect information about planets and their satellites are also called rockets. We hear of rockets in fire-works also. Whatever be the context in which the word rocket is used, one thing is certain that all the rockets function on the same principle. A rocket works according to the Newton's third law of motion. According to this law, 'to every action there is an equal and opposite reaction'. The gases formed by the burning of fuels inside the rocket chamber come out of the nozzle and produce a great force. As a reaction to this, the rocket gets the necessary push to move forward. Do you know how the rocket was developed?

The story of the development of the rocket starts with China. It was not invented by any single scientist. Its development took a very long time. In the year 1232, the Chinese used the arrows of flying fire in the wars against the Mongols. These arrows were also a kind of rockets. By 1275, rockets came to be in use in India, England, Arabian countries, Germany and France etc. During the early 1800s, Colonel William Congreve of the British Army developed rockets which were used in every war thereafter. In 1926 Robert H.

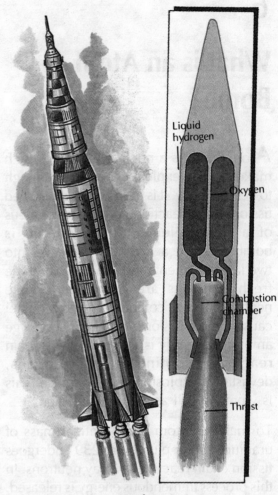

Rocket

Goddard of America developed liquid propelled rockets. Goddard today is known as "The Father of Modern Rocketry."

High speed rockets were developed for space explorations. The space Age began on October 4, 1957 when Russia launched the first satellite, Sputnik I. Today we have solid and liquid propellent rockets, electric and nuclear rockets. For space applications, scientists are using multistage rockets. ○○○

6

What is an Atom Bomb?

Atom bomb is a nuclear weapon which makes a huge explosion powerful enough to destroy a city. It is based on uncontrolled fission chain reaction. When the nucleus of a heavy element like uranium is bombarded by a neutron, it breaks into two large fragments and either two or three fresh neutrons are produced. These neutrons further collide with other nuclei causing more fissions. In this process large amount of energy is released. If the chain reaction continues, tremendous, devastating explosion will take place. This is what we call as atomic explosion.

To make an atom bomb critical mass of uranium-235 or plutonium-239 undergoes fission chain reaction by stray neutrons. In this process tremendous energy is released.

Based on fission chain reaction, the first atomic bomb was developed during the second world war by a team of American scientists. The first atomic bomb made of uranium-235 was dropped on August 6, 1945 on Hiroshima and three days later

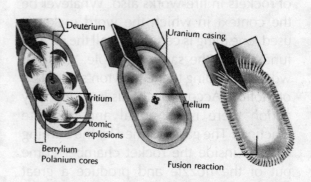

Robert Oppenheimer, the father of Atom Bomb

the second bomb based on plutonium was dropped on Nagasaki (Japan). Those have been most tragic events in the history of mankind. Destruction caused by these bombs ended second world war.

After this Russia, Britain, China and France also tested their atom bombs.   OOO

7

What is a radar and how does it work?

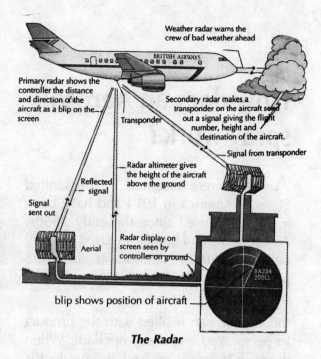

The Radar

The labels in the figure read:
- Weather radar warns the crew of bad weather ahead
- BRITISH AIRWAYS
- Primary radar shows the controller the distance and direction of the aircraft as a blip on the screen
- Secondary radar makes a transponder on the aircraft send out a signal giving the flight number, height and destination of the aircraft.
- Transponder
- Signal from transponder
- Radar altimeter gives the height of the aircraft above the ground
- Reflected signal
- Signal sent out
- Aerial
- Radar display on screen seen by controller on ground
- BA234 200LL
- blip shows position of aircraft

The word 'radar' is an acronym for 'radio detection and ranging'. It is, in fact, an electronic device by which one can detect and measure an invisible flying object's distance and speed. It can work efficiently under all weather conditions such as fog, mist, smoke, snow-fall, storm, cyclone, rains etc. Due to these reasons it is used in the control-room for the guidance of aeroplanes.

The radar works on the principle of 'echo'. The sound waves reflected by some obstacle produce an echo. Similarly, radio waves which are electromagnetic in nature also get reflected when they encounter some obstacle in their path. This property of radio waves was discovered by scientists in 1930. Using this property, in 1935 five radar centres were established in America. Major developments in the field of radars took place during the Second World War. These rendered a great help in detecting the enemy bombers. Since then, many kinds of radar have been developed for peaceful uses also. Now, there are radars which help in controlling and guiding the path of unmanned space crafts. Radars giving information relating to weather are also available.

Do you know how radar works? Radars make use of radio-waves, similar to those used in radio broadcasting. However, the radio-waves used in radar have higher frequencies. They are called micro-waves. The speed of these waves is equal to that of light i.e. 3×10^8 metres (186000 miles) per second. The radar centre has a transmitter which sends out radio waves with the help of an antenna towards the object. It also has a receiver which receives the radio waves reflected by the object. This receiver has a screen which shows the object's position in the sky.

The time taken by the radio-waves in going from the transmitter to the object and in coming back to the receiver is recorded by radar. By multiplying this time with the velocity of light we get twice the distance between the radar and the object. This is how the distance of the object is determined. The radar has automatic instruments which perform all these functions. Initially, radars used to be very big in size, but now there are ones which are even smaller than our palms. OOO

8

How does an Aerosol spray work?

Aerosols were patented in the United States of America in 1914 and have been increasingly used since the early 1950s. Aerosol cans and bottles are used to spray paints, perfumes, deodorants, furniture polish, oven cleaner, pesticides and many other liquid products.

Initially the can is filled with the product to be sprayed and the propellant. When the push button is pressed, the product is forced up the dip tube and comes out as spray from the hole in the top. The top hole is very narrow and causes the liquid to break up into a fine, mist-like spray. Inside the can, the propellant is a gas under pressure usually a chlorofluorocarbon which forces the liquid in the tube to the top. However, concern about the damaging effects that chlorofluoro carbons have on the earth's ozone layer has forced scientists to look for alternatives. The top of the can

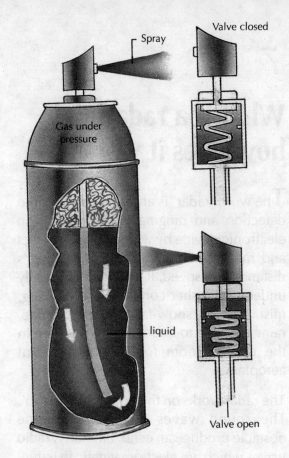

The functioning of Aerosal

contains a valve with a spring that closes the value when the top is released.

Because an aerosol can contains a gas under pressure, it is dangerous to heat the can as it may explode.   OOO

9

How does an Electric Typewriter work?

Electric typewriters are increasingly replacing the mechanical typewriters. The

first commercial typewriter was produced in 1874 by Christopher Latham Sholes. It was produced by Remington company of USA. The first electric typewriter was marketed in the mid 1930s.

An electric typewriter along with its functional diagram is shown in the figures. An electric typewriter involved less manual labour as compared to the old mechanical machines. The mechanism of this typewriter is more efficient.

When a key (1) is pressed, a cam (2) makes contact with a drive roller (3) powered by an electric motor (4) The cam is propelled upwards with an even force, causing the cam lever (5) to move back. This makes the upwards movement of the appropriate type bar. (6) The paper is wound on a cylinder which moves along one character at a time during typing. A typing ribbon is forced against the paper by the metal bar, so printing a letter on the paper. As the type bar falls back, the carriage moves one character space to the left. The force of the typing strokes does not depend on the pressure applied by the typist so the results are more even. At the end of a line the typist presses a key that shifts the carriage to the right and at the same time rotates the cylinder, carrying the paper to the beginning of the next line.

Electronic typewriters are move sophisticated than electric typewriters. Based on microchip control they are usually very quiet to use and their action is faster since they contain less moving parts. They offer more functions specially they have memory that allows user to make corrections.

The word processor while retaining the advantages of the electronic typewriter keyboard has replaced the movement of the carriage and cylinder by the movement of a cursor on the screen. This means that mistakes can be erased and passages added, removed or repositioned before the matter is typed on the paper.   ooo

An electric typewriter

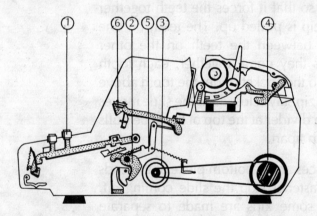

By depressing a key (1) corresponding to the character to be typed, a cam (2) makes contact with a drive roller (3) powered by a constant-speed motor (4) The cam is propelled upwards with an even force, causing the cam lever (5) to move back. This results in the upward movement of the appropriate type bar (6) The paper is wound on a cylinder or platen, which moves along one character at a time during typing.

10

How does a Zip Fastener work?

Zip fastener is a fastening device in which two rows of teeth and sockets are brought together so that they interlock. Metal zips have lines of tiny teeth, while plastic zips contain small loops on each side. When you pull the slide of the zip fastener up, it pushes the teeth or loop together. The first zip was invented by Whitcomb Judson in 1893.

Beneath each tooth in a metal zip fastener is a small socket. The slide is narrow at the bottom so that it forces the teeth together as the zip is pulled up. The teeth on one side fit between the teeth on the other side. As they come together, each tooth slips into the socket under the tooth above and the zip stays closed. As the slide moves down, a divider at the top of the slide pulls the teeth apart.

Top pieces and a bottom piece at the ends of the fastener stop the slide coming off, though some zips are made to separate completely by pulling one line of teeth out of the bottom piece. Plastic zips have two spiral coils instead of lines of teeth but their working principle is the same. ○○○

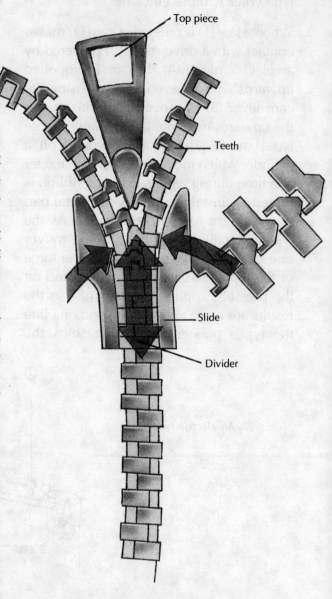

Top piece

Teeth

Slide

Divider

The zip fastener: an improved method of fastening garments

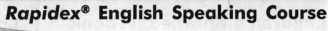

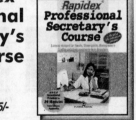

Demy size, pp: 365

Demy size, pp: 282

Demy size, pp: 180

Demy size, pp: 142

Demy size, pp: 184

Demy size, pp: 160

Demy size, pp: 152

Demy size, pp: 136

Demy size, pp: 264

Demy size, pp: 144

Demy size, pp: 270

Big size, pp: 248

Demy size, pp: 236

Demy size, pp: 160

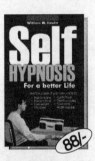

Demy size, pp: 184

Demy size, pp: 107

Demy size, pp: 272

Demy size, pp: 222

Big size, pp: 264

Demy size, pp: 120

Demy size, pp: 120

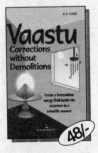

Demy size, pp: 92

Demy size, pp: 144

Discover the world of
Pustak
Mahal
Books
Visit our
website:
www.pustakmahal.com

68/-

60/-

48/-

48/-

68/-

88/-

Demy size, pp: 160
Also available in Hindi
and Bangla

Demy size, pp: 136
Also available in Hindi

Demy size, pp: 64

Demy size, pp: 80
Also available in Hindi

Demy size, pp: 156

Demy size, pp: 290

96/-

68/-

80/-

60/-

120/-

80/-

Demy size, pp: 184

Demy size, pp: 166

Demy size, pp: 216

Demy size, pp: 240

Demy size, pp: 304

Demy size, pp: 180

60/-

80/-

80/-

68/-

80/-

60/-

Demy size, pp: 128

Demy size, pp: 218

Demy size, pp: 174

Demy size, pp: 176

Demy size, pp: 140

Demy size, pp: 140

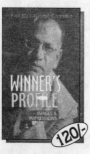

60/-

120/-

68/-

68/-

80/-

80/-

Demy size, pp: 155

Demy size, pp: 128

Demy size, pp: 128

Demy size, pp: 176

Demy size, pp: 136

Demy size, pp: 176

POSTAGE: RS. 15 TO 25/- EACH

31 Mantras for Personality Development
60/-

Demy size, pp: 104

The Portrait of a Complete Man
80/-

Demy size, pp: 176

The 4-Lane Expressway to STRESS MANAGEMENT
68/-

Demy size, pp: 112

The Book of Etiquette and Manners
68/-

Demy size, pp: 136

Make Marriage a Success & Live Happily Ever After
80/-

Demy size, pp: 176

How to integrate the self
80/-

Demy size, pp: 112

The World's Best Thought-Provoking JOKES
80/-

Demy size, pp: 176

The Portrait of a Perfect WOMAN
80/-

Demy size, pp: 128

SECRETS OF HAPPINESS
Tanushree Podder
80/-

Demy size, pp: 192

Hello! Just married or about to marry?
80/-

Demy size, pp: 144

365 GEMS FOR HOLISTIC LIVING
ALAN COHEN
195/-

Demy size, pp: 376
(Hardbound)

The Art of Happy Living
In Press

Demy size, pp: 168

freedom from thought
New
96/-

Demy size, pp: 184

TALES OF WISDOM
60/-

Demy size, pp: 144

50 Moral Tales ...from The Gurukul
68/-

Big size, pp: 112

The Portrait of a Super Student
80/-

Demy size, pp: 144
(Double Colour)

7 Mantras to Excel in EXAMS
80/-

Demy size, pp: 144

Boost Your Brain-Power
Dr G Francis Xavier, PhD
96/-

Demy size, pp: 144

Immortal Sayings
96/-

Demy size, pp: 192

2000 TITBITS & SATIRES TO MAKE YOU GRIN, SMIRK & LAUGH
68/-

Demy size, pp: 176

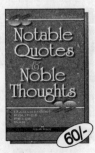

Notable Quotes & Noble Thoughts
60/-

Demy size, pp: 96

A Treasury of Inspirational Thoughts
68/-

Demy size, pp: 144

The Book of Uncommon Quips & Quotations
80/-

Demy size, pp: 128

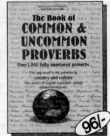

The Book of COMMON & UNCOMMON PROVERBS
96/-

Big size, pp: 128

POSTAGE: RS. 15 TO 25/- EACH

Become a Successful SPEAKER

68/-

Demy size, pp: 136

SUCCESS SECRETS — A COMMON-SENSE GUIDE TO LIFELONG ACHIEVEMENT

120/-

Demy size, pp: 256

Youngsters' Guide for PERSONAL DEVELOPMENT

68/-

Demy size, pp: 120

You too can Become Rich

80/-

Demy size, pp: 128

SMART MEMORY — Techniques to Improve Memory

68/-

Demy size, pp: 138

How to Motivate Others — to turn them into super performers

80/-

Big size, pp: 128

SOLVE YOUR PROBLEMS — The Birbal Way

68/-

Demy size, pp: 200

TEENS TO TWENTIES — A guide for youngsters

68/-

Demy size, pp: 120

Don't just be Successful ...Be more than Successful

68/-

Demy size, pp: 120

Making Friends and doing business in Europe

96/-

Demy size, pp: 288

The Street Smart Salesman — Making Opportunities Happen

88/-

Demy size, pp: 208

How to be a favourite with your BOSS

80/-

Big size, pp: 106

20 Keys for SUCCESS in JOB & CAREER

80/-

Demy size, pp: 144

GREAT SPEAKERS AREN'T BORN — The Complete Guide to Winning Presentations

88/-

Demy size, pp: 192

Skills for Excellence

88/-

Demy size, pp: 176

How to be the Complete Professional Salesperson — Robert L. Shook

120/-

Demy size, pp: 232

HOW TO MAKE A GREAT PRESENTATION in 2 hours — FRANK PAOLO

80/-

Demy size, pp: 212

LET'S GET RESULTS NOT EXCUSES!

195/-

Demy size, pp: 240

U.S. VISA MADE EASY — a practical guide

220/-

Big size, pp: 188

MARKETING WITH SPEECHES AND SEMINARS — Your Key to More Clients and Referrals

80/-

Demy size, pp: 176

Directory of Management Courses in India

60/-

Demy size, pp: 392

BEGINNERS' GUIDE TO JOURNALISM

80/-

Demy size, pp: 128

Study & Immigration in U.S.A

95/-

Demy size, pp: 128

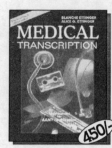

MEDICAL TRANSCRIPTION

450/-

Big size, pp: 472

POSTAGE: RS. 15 TO 25/- EACH

New

Bite-sized bits on
Common-sense Management

Small in size but packed with powerful practical insights on most aspects of management

Gerard Assey

150/-

Demy size, pp: 100

New

Mastering Salary Negotiations

How to skilfully negotiate the best remuneration package

96/-

Demy size, pp: 96

WINNING Résumé

How to write an impressive curriculum vitae (CV) that guarantees you an interview call

80/-

Demy size, pp: 136

GROUP DISCUSSION
For Admissions & Jobs

88/-

Demy size, pp: 200

Business Ideas you can turn into Cash

80/-

Demy size, pp: 128

Multiple Career Choices
For Graduate & Post-Graduate Courses

An invaluable database of courses at colleges, universities and institutions across India

135/-

Big size, pp: 280

Secrets of Leadership

Insights from the Panchatantra

Learn leadership qualities through the 101 tales from the Panchatantra.

80/-

Demy size, pp: 136

Sure Success in Interviews

The most comprehensive one-source guide for succeeding in interviews.

80/-

Demy size, pp: 152

QUIZ BOOKS

MATHEMATICS QUIZ BOOK

48/-

Demy size, pp: 216

Environment Quiz Book

48/-

Demy size, pp: 176

ASTRONOMY QUIZ BOOK

48/-

Demy size, pp: 208

BIRDS & ANIMALS QUIZ BOOK

60/-

Big size, pp: 128

MEDICAL QUIZ BOOK

48/-

Demy size, pp: 192

Electronics & Computer Quiz Book

48/-

Demy size, pp: 260

HISTORY Quiz Book

48/-

Demy size, pp: 232

QUIZ TIME

Over 1100 Quizzes on SCIENCE, HISTORY, GEOGRAPHY, LITERATURE, FILM & SPORTS, ENVIRONMENT, AWARDS & HONOURS, CURRENT AFFAIRS & GENERAL KNOWLEDGE

80/-

Big size, pp: 208

SCIENCE QUIZ BOOK
1001 Questions and Answers

48/-

Demy size, pp: 192

Over 4000 Quizzes 163 Topics
GLOBAL QUIZ BOOK

Films & Entertainment • People and Places • Famous & Notables • Biology & Human Body • Books & Authors • Art & Heritage • Awards & Achievements • Science & Inventions • Religion & Mythology • ...And many more

96/-

Demy size, pp: 256

General Science, Physics, Chemistry and Biology
4000 Quizzes
All Illustrated

80/-

Demy size, pp: 240

Discover India Series
TAMIL NADU Quiz Book

40/-

Demy size, pp: 160

Pre-School Primers

MY FIRST STEP OF **ALPHABET**

मेरा पहला कदम **क ख ग**

MY FIRST STEP OF **NUMBERS**

MY FIRST STEP OF **NURSERY RHYMES**

MY FIRST STEP OF **BIRDS AND ANIMALS**

MY FIRST STEP OF **VEGETABLES AND FRUITS**

My first step of:
• Alphabet
• क • ख • ग
• Numbers
• Nursery Rhymes
• Birds & Animals
• Vegetables & Fruits

Price: Rs. 30/- each

PICTURE BOOK OF **ALPHABETS**

36/-

All books fully coloured and illustrated. Can be cleaned wiped off.

POSTAGE: RS. 15 TO 25/- EACH

7

HEALTH, NUTRITION, YOGA, BEAUTY & BODY CARE

60/-

Demy size, pp: 176
Also available in Hindi

48/-

Demy size, pp: 112
Also available in Hindi

40/-

Demy size, pp: 112
Also available in Hindi

48/-

Demy size, pp: 128
Also available in Hindi

60/-

Demy size, pp: 120

60/-

Big size, pp: 112

80/-

Demy size, pp: 200

60/-

Demy size, pp: 128

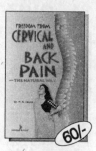

60/-

Demy size, pp: 128

60/-

Demy size, pp: 100

80/-

Demy size, pp: 224

60/-

Big size, pp: 128
Also available in Hindi

68/-

Demy size, pp: 192

60/-

Demy size, pp: 120

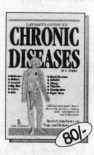

80/-

Demy size, pp: 176

80/-

Demy size, pp: 126

60/-

Demy size, pp: 124

68/-

Big size, pp: 144

68/-

Demy size, pp: 160

68/-

Demy size, pp: 144

40/-

Demy size, pp: 112

96/-

Demy size, pp: 152

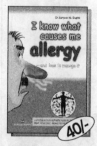

40/-

Demy size, pp: 96

75/-

Big size, pp: 144

POSTAGE: RS. 15 TO 25/- EACH

HEALTH, NUTRITION, YOGA, BEAUTY & BODY CARE

Demy size, pp: 120

Demy size, pp: 192

Demy size, pp: 128

Demy size, pp: 144

Big size, pp: 428

Big size, pp: 228

Demy size, pp: 152

Vol-I: pp: 140 • Rs. 96/-
Vol-II: pp: 224 • Rs. 135/-

Demy size, pp: 128

Demy size, pp: 224

Big size, pp: 232

Big size, pp: 152

Demy size, pp: 96

Demy size, pp: 240

Demy size, pp: 136

Demy size, pp: 116

Big size, pp: 224

Big size, pp: 224

Demy size, pp: 224

Demy size, pp: 224

Demy size, pp: 120

Demy size, pp: 136

Big size, pp: 208

Big size, pp: 184

POSTAGE: RS. 15 TO 25/- EACH

Youthful Forever

80/-

Demy size, pp: 248

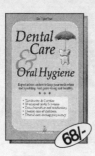

Dental Care & Oral Hygiene

68/-

Demy size, pp: 136

Slim & Smart Body

60/-

Demy size, pp: 128

Home-made Herbal Cosmetics

68/-

Demy size, pp: 128

Your Diet After 50

68/-

Demy size, pp: 152

FIT & FINE IN BODY & MIND

90/-

Big size, pp: 232

You are What you Eat

80/-

Demy size, pp: 184

Better SEX The Herbal Way

68/-

Demy size, pp: 128

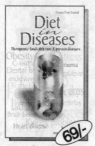

Diet in Diseases

69/-

Demy size, pp: 104

Laughter the secret of good health

60/-

Demy size, pp: 120

Unicorn Safe-n-Sure Weight Loss Programme

96/-

Demy size, pp: 132

The Magic of Massage

96/-

Big size, pp: 176

Ayurveda for All

120/-

Big size, pp: 224

OVER 1000 HEALTH HINTS FOR ONE & ALL

80/-

Big size, pp: 168

Fact Books in Herbs

Brahmi · Ashwagandha · Spirulina · Vilayati imli · Salai guggal · Amla

Price: Rs. 30/- each
Postage: Rs. 10/- each

Demy size
Pages: 32 each

Popular Science & Science Tricks

71 +10 New Science Projects Self-learning Kit

120/-

Big size • pp: 120
(With CD)
Also available in Hindi

Electronics Projects for Beginners

96/-

Big size • pp: 196

101 Science Games

48/-

Big size • pp: 120

101 SCIENCE EXPERIMENTS

48/-

Big size • pp: 120

Bathroom Science Tricks

36/-

Big size • pp: 104

Kitchen Science Tricks

36/-

Big size • pp: 104

POSTAGE: RS. 15 TO 25/- EACH

SPIRITUAL HEALING, REIKI & ALTERNATIVE THERAPIES

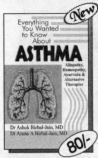     

Everything You Wanted to Know About **ASTHMA** — 80/-
Demy size, pp: 168

Soul HEALING — 88/-
Demy size, pp: 280

CHAKRA WORKOUT For Body, Mind & Spirit — 88/-
Demy size, pp: 240

Healing the Past For a **Vibrant Future** — 68/-
Demy size, pp: 180

Self-Defence against **psychic attacks & evil spirits** — 96/-
Demy size, pp: 242

CHAKRA & KUNDALINI WORKBOOK — 96/-
Demy size, pp: 264

  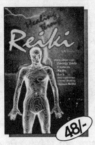   

A Beginner's Guide to **ACUPRESSURE** (SHIATSU Technique) — 36/-
Demy size, pp: 64

Auras See Them in only 60 Seconds! — 80/-
Demy size, pp: 144

Reiki — 48/-
Demy size, pp: 104

TAOIST & YOGA CHI-KUNG — 108/-
Demy size, pp: 304

The Magic of *Aromatherapy* — 108/-
Demy size, pp: 264

The **ACUPRESSURE HANDBOOK** — 135/-
Big size, pp: 264

COLOUR THERAPY — Miracle of Sun Rays — 40/-
Demy size, pp: 84

the healing touch of *Reiki* — 68/-
Demy size, pp: 112

MASTER APPROACHES TO **NEW AGE ALTERNATIVE THERAPIES** — 80/-
Demy size, pp: 200

WATER A Miracle Therapy — 68/-
Demy size, pp: 112

Magneto Therapy The miraculous healing power — 68/-
Demy size, pp: 128

The Practical Book of **REIKI** Healing Through Universal Lifeforce Energy — 96/-
Big size, pp: 168

The miracle of **Music Therapy** — 80/-
Demy size, pp: 144

21 Power Tools of **Reiki** — 60/-
Demy size, pp: 136

Magic Therapy of COLOURS Holistic healing through colours — 60/-
Demy size, pp: 128

Healing Heart Disease Naturally — 96/-
Demy size, pp: 200

Relaxation Techniques — 195/-
Demy size, pp: 272

The Healing Power of **Mudras** The Yoga of the hands — 68/-
Demy size, pp: 112

POSTAGE: RS. 15 TO 25/- EACH

11

DICTIONARIES & ENCYCLOPEDIAS

40/-
Big size, pp: 48

60/-
Demy size, pp: 136

120/-
Big size, pp: 231

72/-
Big size, pp: 48

48/-
Demy size, pp: 192

380/-
Big size, pp: 518

360/-
Big size, pp: 384

120/-
Demy size, pp: 344

60/-
Demy size, pp: 128

100/-
Also available in Hindi

68/-
Demy size, pp: 352

50/-
Demy size, pp: 452

88/-
Demy size, pp: 452

68/-
Demy size, pp: 128

24/-
Demy size, pp: 152

60/-
Demy size, pp: 104

48/-
Demy size, pp: 128

68/-
Demy size, pp: 232

Postage: Rs. 15 to 20/- each

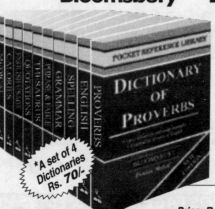

Bloomsbury Dictionaries

- Dictionary of Phrase & Fable
- English Thesaurus
- Spelling Dictionary
- Dictionary of English Usage
- Medical Dictionary
- Dictionary of Calories
- English Dictionary*
- Dictionary of Grammar*
- Dictionary of Proverbs*
- Dictionary of Quotations*

*A set of 4 Dictionaries Rs. 70/-

Pocket size • Pages: 256
Price: Rs. 30/- each • Postage: Rs. 10/- each

COMPUTER BOOKS

Big size • pp: 224
Also available in Hindi

125/-

Big size • pp: 504
(FREE CD-ROM, SMS Joke
Book & Mouse Pad).
Also available in Hindi

175/-

Big size • pp: 448

175/-

Big size • pp: 520

195/-

Big size • pp: 224

60/-

Big size • pp: 144

95/-

Big size • pp: 136

90/-

Big size • pp: 264

68/-

Big size • pp: 360

195/-

Big size • pp: 192

68/-

Big size • pp: 416

195/-

Big size • pp: 444

225/-

Big size • pp: 392

225/-

Big size • pp: 184

90/-

Big size • pp: 252

125/-

Demy size • pp: 296

140/-

Demy size • pp: 164

120/-

Rapidex Straight to the point series

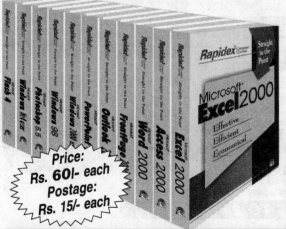

Microsoft Excel
2000

Access 2000

Word 2000

FrontPage 2000

Outlook 2000

PowerPoint 2000

Windows 2000
User

Windows 98

PhotoShop 5.5

WindowsNT4 User

Flash 4

Price:
Rs. 60/- each
Postage:
Rs. 15/- each

Rapidex Condensed Users Guides

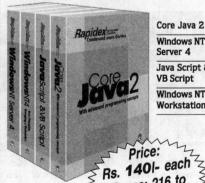

Core Java 2

Windows NT
Server 4

Java Script &
VB Script

Windows NT 4
Workstation

Price:
Rs. 140/- each
Pages: 216 to
316 each

FUN, FACTS, HUMOUR, MAGIC & HOBBIES

Strange But True Facts

80/-

Demy size, pp: 184

Fun with Numbers

40/-

Demy size, pp: 115
also available in Hindi

101 BRAIN TEASERS

48/-

Demy size, pp: 152

Incredible But True

36/-

Demy size, pp: 112
also available in Hindi

501 FASCINATING FACTS

40/-

Demy size, pp: 104
also available in Hindi,
Bangla, kannada &
Assamese

501 ASTONISHING FACTS

36/-

Demy size, pp: 115
also available in Hindi

How to solve Crossword Puzzles

60/-

Demy size, pp: 104

Amusing Anecdotes on Indian Red Tape

80/-

Demy size, pp: 176

Rib-Tickling JOKES

48/-

Demy size, pp: 128

MEDICAL JOKES & HUMOUR

60/-

Demy size, pp: 152

ARMOUR OF HUMOUR

40/-

Demy size, pp: 128

DEFT DEFINITIONS

48/-

Demy size, pp: 120

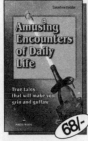

Amusing Encounters of Daily Life

68/-

Demy size, pp: 124

Stories from Panchatantra

60/-

Demy size, pp: 115

(New) The Funniest Tales of Mullah Nasruddin

Pages: 144

(New) 50 WITTIEST TALES OF BIRBAL

48/-

Pages: 120

(New) THE WORLD'S BEST PROFESSIONAL JOKES

60/-

Pages: 200

(New) UNWRITTEN FLAWS OF INDIAN BUREAUCRACY

295/-

Demy size, pp: 248
(Hardbound)

Animal Folk Tales from Around the World

36/-

Big size, pp: 24
Also available in Hindi

MAGIC FOR FUN

36/-

Demy size, pp: 112
also available in Hindi,
Kannada & Marathi

MAGIC for CHILDREN

48/-

Demy size, pp: 112
also available in Hindi

MAGIC for YOU

36/-

Demy size, pp: 112
also available in Hindi

101 MAGIC TRICKS

48/-

Big size, pp: 112
also available in Hindi,
Telugu, bangla & Assamese

HOW TO DRAW CARTOONS

60/-

Demy size, pp: 160

Drawing and Painting Course

48/-

Big size, pp: 120

POSTAGE: RS. 15 TO 25/- EACH

14

COOKERY, HOUSEHOLD & PARENTING

New
COOKING MADE EASY
The ideal cookery book for beginners that goes beyond cooking
60/-
Demy size • pp: 104

OVER **100 FAT-FREE RECIPES**
80/-
Demy size • pp: 120

101 All time **Savoury Snacks**
60/-
Demy size • pp: 102

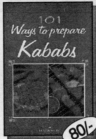
101 **Ways to prepare Kababs**
80/-
Demy size • pp: 136

101 Ways to prepare **Curries**
60/-
Demy size • pp: 140

101 Ways to prepare **Soups & Salads**
60/-
Demy size • pp: 86

MODERN COOKERY BOOK
60/-
Big size • Pages: 144

Wide range of delicious vegetarian and non-vegetarian **Dishes and Desserts** from four corners of India
80/-
Big size • Pages: 86

101 **Mix & Match** recipes with **Vegetables**
60/-
Demy size • Pages: 144

101 **Chinese Recipes**
60/-
Demy size • Pages: 112

Cooking for Diabetics
Diet plays a very important role in any disease, more so in diabetes.
80/-
Demy size • pp: 115

1000 Plus **Household Hints**
96/-
Big size • Pages: 192

HOME HINTS
How to save time and money
40/-
Big size • Pages: 32

FIRST AID FOR EVERY HOME
40/-
Big size • Pages: 32

COOKERY (a set of 4 books)

Cooking Pleasurable
An exciting set of four cookery books covering Indian curries to Chinese recipes, soups to salads & mix & match vegetable dishes.

you save **20%**

Rs 200/-
Pay Rs. **200/-** instead of Rs. 240/- for complete set of 4 books priced Rs. 60/- each

- 101 Mix & Match Recipes with Vegetables
- 101 Chinese Recipes
- 101 Ways to Prepare Curries
- 101 Ways to Prepare Soups & Salads

SPOT CHECK
How to cope with household stains
Nina Grunfeld and Micheal Thomes
40/-
Big size • Pages: 32

HOUSE PLANTS
How to care for your indoor plants
Peter McHoy
40/-
Big size • Pages: 32

Rapidex **HOME MANAGEMENT GUIDE**
150/-
Big size • Pages: 296

Books on PARENTING

How to shape your Kids Better
It is in parent's hands to mould their children into perfection
68/-
Pages: 124

The Art of **Successful Parenting**
68/-
Pages: 140

PRACTICAL PARENTING TIPS
Over 1,500 Helpful Hints for the First Five Years
68/-
Pages: 208

The Joy of Parenting
A comprehensive parenting guide covering infancy to adolescence
80/-
Pages: 144

DISCIPLINE YOUR CHILD WITHOUT SHOUTING or SPANKING
Practical Solutions to the Most Common Pre-school Behaviour Problems
Jerry Wyckoff, Ph.D. and Barbara C.Unell
80/-
Pages: 132

Bringing up a **Dream Child**
Gentle ways to discipline your child
75/-
Pages: 118

Raising a Daughter in 21st Century India From cradle to marriage and after
60/-
PP: 136

15

Religious & Spiritual Books

75/-
Pages: 208

80/-
Pages: 224

48/-
Pages: 104

80/-
Pages: 120

80/-
Pages: 152

96/-
Pages: 132

New
80/-
Pages: 136

New
80/-
Pages: 158

Postage: Rs. 10/- to 20/- each

Furniture Catalogue, Gates, Grills, Windows, Railings....

Exclusive pictorial handbook for practical designing suiting individual tastes.

- New Furniture Catalogue **120/-**
- New Steel Furniture Catalogue **195/-**
- Gates, Grills & Railings Sets **60/-**
- Designs of Windows **60/-**
- Designs of Gates **60/-**
- Designs of Railings **60/-**
- Top Design of Windows, Grills and Rolling Shutters **60/-**
- More & More Designs of Gates, Grills Railings & Staircases **90/-**
- How best to Plan & Build Your Home **120/-**

Postage: Rs. 10/- to 20/- each

16

World Famous Series

Discoveries

Great Lives (3 vols.)

Strange Mysteries

Ghosts

Civilizations

Great Treasurers

Notorious Women

Scientists

Unsolves Mysteries

Anecdotes

Adventures

Mythologies

Prophecies & Predictions

Supernatural Mysteries

Romances of Great People

Famous Indians of 20th Century
Pages: 224

The World's Greatest Seers & Philosophers
Pages: 142

Demy size • Pages: 120-160 in each Price: Rs. **48/-** each
Postage: 15/- each
Postage free on 6 or more books
All books in Hindi also
Four books in Bangla & Kannada